JOYFUL STUFFED [
& ANIMALS

ONDORI

CONTENTS

★ Copyright © 1985 Ondorisha Publishers Ltd., All Rights Reserved.
★ Published by Ondorisha Publishers Ltd. 32 Nishigoken-cho, Shinjuku-ku,
Tokyo 162, Japan.
★ Sole Overseas Distributor: Japan Publications Trading Co., Ltd.
P.O. Box 5030 Tokyo International, Tokyo, Japan.
★ Distributed in the United States by Kodansha International/USA Ltd.
through Harper & Row, Publishers, Inc., 10 East 53rd Street, New York,
New York 10022.
Australia by Bookwise, International, 1 Jeanes Street, Beverley, South Australia
5007, Australia.

10 9 8 7 6 5 4 3 2

ISBN 0-87040-648-5   Printed in Japan

PLAYMATES FROM FAIRY TALES

Doctor Doolittle 1

Instructions on page 2.

Doctor Doolittle ⟵⟹ shown on page 1

You'll Need Felt: 14 cm by 11 cm Cream. 11 cm by 10 cm Olive Green. 12 cm by 9 cm Beige. 14 cm by 8 cm Light Moss Green. 8 cm by 6 cm Brown. Lightweight yarn Dark Brown small amount. 6-strand embroidery floss Yellow Ocher, Dark Brown, Vermilion small amount each. Sewing cotton White, Black small amount each. Bead: 3 of White (small size). 2 of Black (mid size). Small amount of kapok. Glue.

Finished Size 14 cm tall
Cutting
Cut pieces out of fabric with no seam allowance.
Assembly
Unless specified, sew felt pieces with open-buttonhole stitch.
Make body, arms, and hat referring to chart.
Sew head (inserting ears between) and shoes opening left, stuff with kapok, close openings. Sew head, arms, and shoes on body, apply hair on head, secure hat in position. Make nose inserting kapok, make facial features, put clothes on referring to chart.

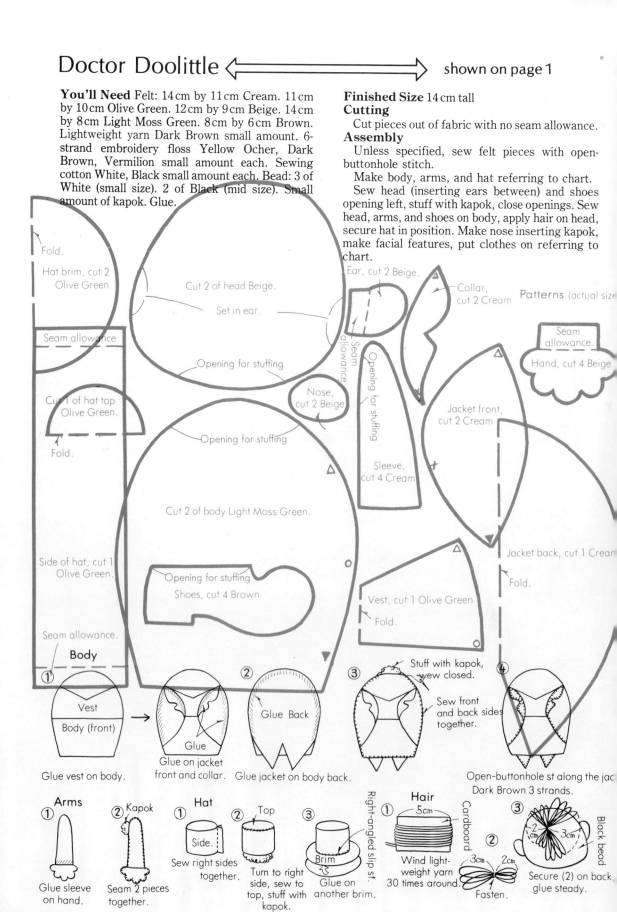

Fold.
Hat brim, cut 2 Olive Green
Seam allowance
Cut 1 of hat top Olive Green.
Fold.
Side of hat, cut 1 Olive Green.
Seam allowance.
Body

Cut 2 of head Beige.
Set in ear.
Opening for stuffing
Nose, cut 2 Beige
Opening for stuffing
Cut 2 of body Light Moss Green.
Opening for stuffing
Shoes, cut 4 Brown

Ear, cut 2 Beige.
Seam allowance
Opening for stuffing
Sleeve, cut 4 Cream
Vest, cut 1 Olive Green
Fold.

Collar, cut 2 Cream
Patterns (actual size)
Seam allowance.
Hand, cut 4 Beige
Jacket front, cut 2 Cream
Jacket back, cut 1 Cream
Fold.

① Vest / Body (front)
Glue vest on body.

Glue
Glue on jacket front and collar.

② Glue Back
Glue jacket on body back.

③ Stuff with kapok, sew closed.
Sew front and back sides together.

④ Open-buttonhole st along the jac
Dark Brown 3 strands.

Arms
① Glue sleeve on hand.
② Kapok / Seam 2 pieces together.

Hat
① Side. / Sew right sides together.
② Top / Turn to right side, sew to top, stuff with kapok.
③ Brim / Glue on another brim.

Right-angled slip st.
Hair
① 5 cm / Cardboard / Wind lightweight yarn 30 times around.
② 3 cm / 2 cm / Fasten.
③ 2 cm / 3 cm / Black bead / Secure (2) on back, glue steady.

2

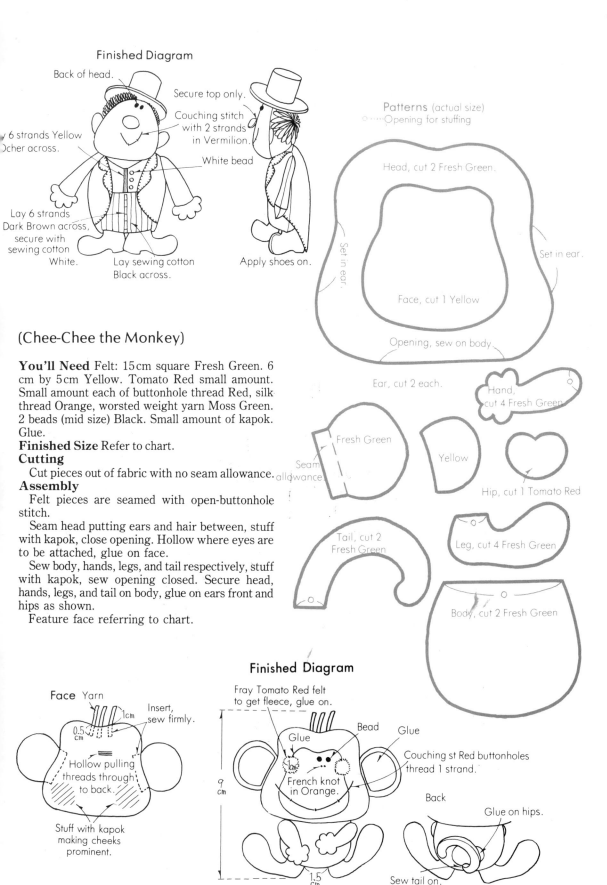

Finished Diagram

Back of head.

Secure top only.

Couching stitch with 2 strands in Vermilion.

6 strands Yellow Ocher across.

White bead

Lay 6 strands Dark Brown across, secure with sewing cotton White.

Lay sewing cotton Black across.

Apply shoes on.

Patterns (actual size)
o······Opening for stuffing

Head, cut 2 Fresh Green.

Set in ear.

Set in ear.

Face, cut 1 Yellow

Opening, sew on body.

Ear, cut 2 each.

Hand, cut 4 Fresh Green.

Fresh Green

Seam allowance.

Yellow

Hip, cut 1 Tomato Red

Tail, cut 2 Fresh Green

Leg, cut 4 Fresh Green

Body, cut 2 Fresh Green

(Chee-Chee the Monkey)

You'll Need Felt: 15cm square Fresh Green. 6 cm by 5cm Yellow. Tomato Red small amount. Small amount each of buttonhole thread Red, silk thread Orange, worsted weight yarn Moss Green. 2 beads (mid size) Black. Small amount of kapok. Glue.

Finished Size Refer to chart.

Cutting
Cut pieces out of fabric with no seam allowance.

Assembly
Felt pieces are seamed with open-buttonhole stitch.

Seam head putting ears and hair between, stuff with kapok, close opening. Hollow where eyes are to be attached, glue on face.

Sew body, hands, legs, and tail respectively, stuff with kapok, sew opening closed. Secure head, hands, legs, and tail on body, glue on ears front and hips as shown.

Feature face referring to chart.

Finished Diagram

Face Yarn

Insert, sew firmly.

0.5 cm   1 cm

Hollow pulling threads through to back.

Stuff with kapok making cheeks prominent.

Fray Tomato Red felt to get fleece, glue on.

Glue

Bead

Glue

Couching st Red buttonholes thread 1 strand.

French knot in Orange.

9 cm

Back

Glue on hips.

1.5 cm

Sew tail on.

Doctor Doolittle 2

Instructions on page 6.

(Whitey the White Mouse)

You'll Need Felt: 20 cm by 18 cm White. Scraps of Pink, Light Pink, Blue. Cotton sewing Black small amount. Bead: 2 of Black (mid size). 1 of Blue (large). Wire #20, 9 cm. Small amount of kapok. Glue.

Finished Size Refer to chart.

Cutting

Cut pieces from fabric with no allowance.

Assembly

Sew face, body, hands, legs, and ears respectively with open-buttonhole st, stuff with kapok, close openings except face opening. Sew gore to face opening, attach teeth as shown.

Secure face, hands, legs, and ears to body, make features referring to chart, sew on tail.

Ear, cut 4 White.

Face, cut 2 White.

Hand, cut 4 White.

Teeth, cut 1 Blue.

Gore, cut 1 Light Pink.

Body, cut 2 White.

Sew on Tail.

Tail, cut 2 White.

Leg, cut 4 White.

Finished Diagram

Black bead

Blue bead

Stuff with kapok, sew in gore, secure teeth.

Pass 2 cm long Black cotton 4 strands through bead, make a knot, apply on top of nose.

Fray Pink felt into fleece, glue on.

8 cm

Attach together putting wire between.

8 cm

Eye, cut 1 each White.

(Jim the Crocodile)

You'll Need Felt: 20 cm by 17 cm Brown. 11 cm by 5 cm Yellow Ocher. Scraps of White, Yellow. Machine thread Black small amount. 2 Black beads (mid size). Small amount of kapok. Glue.

Finished Size Refer to chart.

Cutting

Cut pieces from fabric with no seam allowance.

Assembly

Sew pieces with open-buttonhole stitch, using 1 strand machine thread Black.

Put notches between body pieces, sew together except for mouth and opening.

Join gore pieces, sew to mouth. Stuff kapok into body, close opening.

Sew hands and legs respectively, leaving openings, stuff with kapok, close openings, sew on body.

Apply eyes, attach Yellow pieces on back.

Body, cut 2 Brown.

Seam allowance

Patterns (actual size)

Mark shows opening for stuffing.

Leg, cut 4 Brown.

Hand, cut 4 Braun.

Cut 6 Yellow.

Cut 1 Yellow Ocher.

6

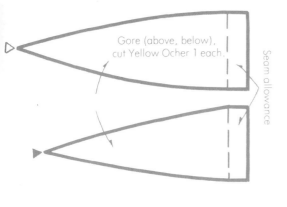

Gore (above, below), cut Yellow Ocher 1 each.

Seam allowance

Sew on gore with right sides together.

Finished Diagram

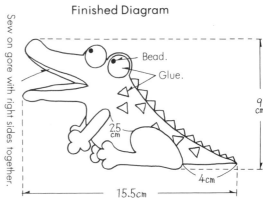

Bead.

Glue.

9 cm

2.5 cm

4 cm

15.5 cm

(Jip the Dog)

You'll Need Felt: 18cm by 15cm Beige. 12cm by 10cm Dark Brown. Pearl floss Red small amount. 2 Black beads (mid size). Small amount of kapok. Glue.

Finished Size Refer to chart.

Cutting

Cut pieces out from fabric with no seam allowance.

Assembly

Felt pieces are sewn with open-buttonhole stitch.

Sew face, body, hands, and legs leaving opening in each to stuff with kapok, close opening.

Sew Dark Brown and Beige ears together. Sew tail, stuff with kapok.

Secure face, hands, legs, and tail on body, sew on ears folding top edge as shown.

Make facial features referring to chart.

Patterns (actual size)

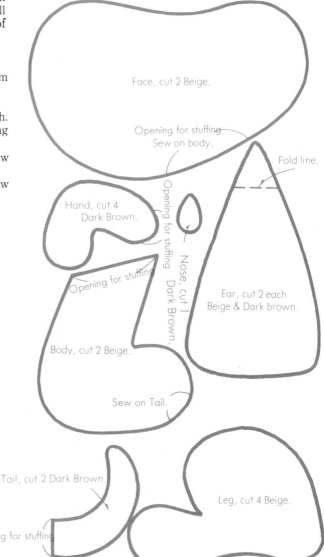

Face, cut 2 Beige.

Opening for stuffing Sew on body.

Fold line.

Hand, cut 4 Dark Brown.

Opening for stuffing

Nose, cut 1 Dark Brown.

Opening for stuffing Dark Brown.

Ear, cut 2 each Beige & Dark brown.

Body, cut 2 Beige.

Sew on Tail.

Tail, cut 2 Dark Brown.

Leg, cut 4 Beige.

Opening for stuffing

Opening for stuffing

Finished Diagram

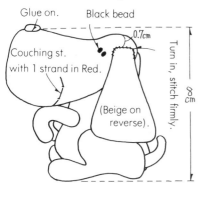

Glue on.

Black bead

0.7cm

Couching st. with 1 strand in Red.

Turn in, stitch firmly.

8 cm

(Beige on reverse).

Instructions for parrot, see page 100.

Doctor Doolittle 2

Instructions on page 10.

(Captain Blossom)

You'll Need Felt: 20 cm square Black. 13 cm by 8 cm Purple. 11 cm by 8 cm Beige. Scraps of Brown, Red. 6-strand Black embroidery floss, Red buttonhole thread, small amount each. Bead (mid size): Black, White Pearl 2 each. Wire #20, 20 cm. Floral tape Olive Green small amount. White frill (see photo) 2.5 cm wide by 7 cm. Sport weight ring yarn Brown small amount. Small amount of kapok. Glue.

Finished Size 15 cm tall

Cutting

Cut pieces from fabric with no allowance.

Assembly

Felt pieces are sewn with open-buttonhole stitch.

Make body referring to chart. Make hat and arms as for Dr. Doolittle on page 2. Sew head (inserting ears) and shoes, opening left, stuff with kapok, close opening.

Secure head, arms, and shoes on body, sew frill in position.

Seam nose putting kapok between, secure top to position, make features on face.

Make beard, secure in position, apply hat on head. Make a whip, sew on hands as shown.

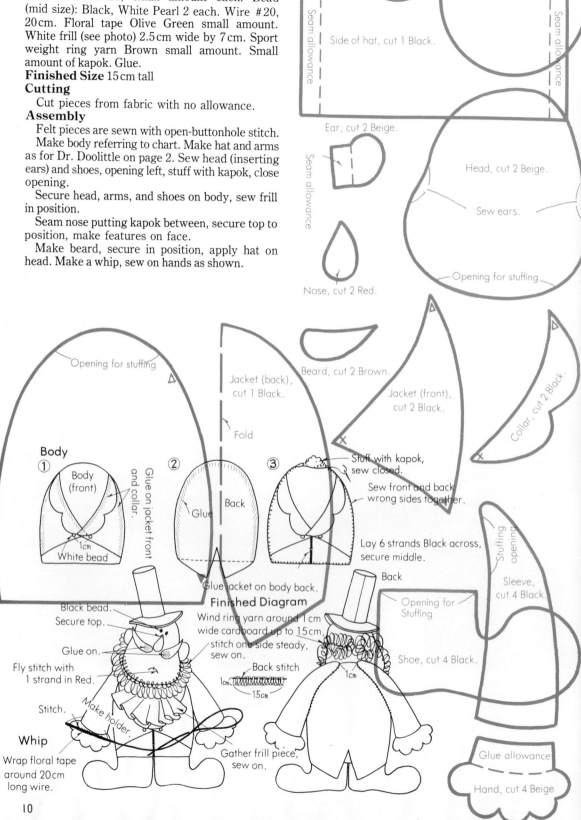

Patterns (actual size)

Top of hat, cut 1 Black.

Brim of hat, cut 2 Black.

Side of hat, cut 1 Black.

Seam allowance

Seam allowance

Seam allowance

Ear, cut 2 Beige.

Head, cut 2 Beige.

Sew ears.

Opening for stuffing

Nose, cut 2 Red.

Opening for stuffing

Jacket (back), cut 1 Black.

Beard, cut 2 Brown.

Jacket (front), cut 2 Black.

Collar, cut 2 Black.

Fold

Body

① Body (front)

② Back

Glue

Glue on jacket front and collar.

③ Stuff with kapok, sew closed.

Sew front and back wrong sides together.

Lay 6 strands Black across, secure middle.

Stuffing opening

Sleeve, cut 4 Black.

1 cm

White bead

Glue jacket on body back.

Finished Diagram

Back

Opening for Stuffing

Black bead. Secure top.

Glue on.

Fly stitch with 1 strand in Red.

Stitch.

Make holder.

Whip

Wrap floral tape around 20 cm long wire.

Wind ring yarn around 1 cm wide cardboard up to 15 cm, stitch one side steady, sew on.

Back stitch

1 cm ——— 15 cm

Back

1 cm

Shoe, cut 4 Black.

Gather frill piece, sew on.

Glue allowance

Hand, cut 4 Beige.

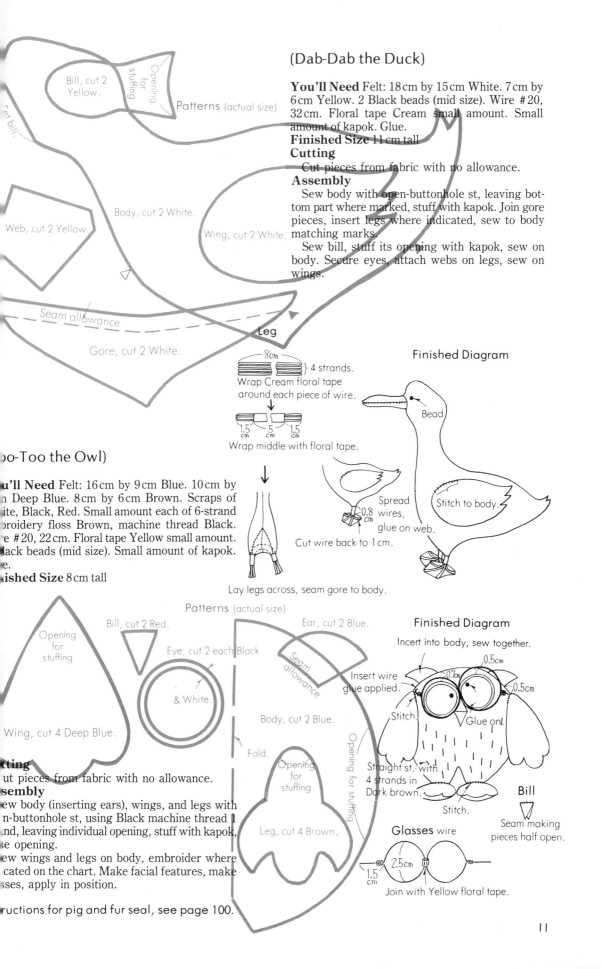

Bill, cut 2 Yellow.

Opening for stuffing

Patterns (actual size)

cut bill.

Web, cut 2 Yellow.

Body, cut 2 White.

Wing, cut 2 White.

Seam allowance

Gore, cut 2 White.

Leg

(Dab-Dab the Duck)

You'll Need Felt: 18cm by 15cm White. 7cm by 6cm Yellow. 2 Black beads (mid size). Wire #20, 32cm. Floral tape Cream small amount. Small amount of kapok. Glue.

Finished Size 11cm tall

Cutting

Cut pieces from fabric with no allowance.

Assembly

Sew body with open-buttonhole st, leaving bottom part where marked, stuff with kapok. Join gore pieces, insert legs where indicated, sew to body matching marks.

Sew bill, stuff its opening with kapok, sew on body. Secure eyes, attach webs on legs, sew on wings.

8cm } 4 strands.
Wrap Cream floral tape around each piece of wire.

1.5 cm 5 cm 1.5 cm
Wrap middle with floral tape.

Cut wire back to 1cm.

Spread wires, glue on web. 0.8 cm

Lay legs across, seam gore to body.

Finished Diagram

Bead

Stitch to body.

(Hoo-Too the Owl)

You'll Need Felt: 16cm by 9cm Blue. 10cm by ? Deep Blue. 8cm by 6cm Brown. Scraps of ?ite, Black, Red. Small amount each of 6-strand ?roidery floss Brown, machine thread Black. ?re #20, 22cm. Floral tape Yellow small amount. ?lack beads (mid size). Small amount of kapok. ?e.

?ished Size 8cm tall

Patterns (actual size)

Opening for stuffing

Bill, cut 2 Red.

Eye, cut 2 each Black

& White.

Wing, cut 4 Deep Blue.

Ear, cut 2 Blue.

Seam allowance

Body, cut 2 Blue.

Fold.

Opening for stuffing

Opening for stuffing

Leg, cut 4 Brown.

?tting

?ut pieces from fabric with no allowance.

?sembly

?ew body (inserting ears), wings, and legs with ?n-buttonhole st, using Black machine thread ?nd, leaving individual opening, stuff with kapok, ?e opening.

?ew wings and legs on body, embroider where ?cated on the chart. Make facial features, make ?ses, apply in position.

?ructions for pig and fur seal, see page 100.

Finished Diagram

Incert into body, sew together.

Insert wire glue applied.

0.7cm 0.5cm
0.5cm

Stitch

Glue onl.

Straight st. with 4 strands in Dark brown.

Stitch.

Bill

Seam making pieces half open.

Glasses wire

2.5cm
1.5 cm
Join with Yellow floral tape.

11

Mary Poppins

Instructions on page 14.

Mary Poppins ⟨⟨===⟩⟩ shown on pages 12—13

You'll Need Jersey: 50 cm wide by 10 cm. 36 cm wide by 8 cm White. 27 cm wide by 6.5 cm Beige. Felt: 5 cm square Black. 5.5 cm by 2.5 cm White. Lightweight yarn Brown small amount. White cotton lace 4.5 cm wide by 14 cm. Black frill (see photo) 2.5 cm wide by 34 cm. White braid 0.8 cm wide by 11 cm. Wire #14, 13 cm. Bead: 2 of Charcoal Gray (mid size). 1 of Red (small size). 6-strand embroidery floss Black, Red small amount each. Cardboard. 7 g. kapok. 4 cm square pebble. Glue.

Finished Size 16 cm tall

Cutting
Cut jersey with 1 cm seam allowance, felt with no allowance.

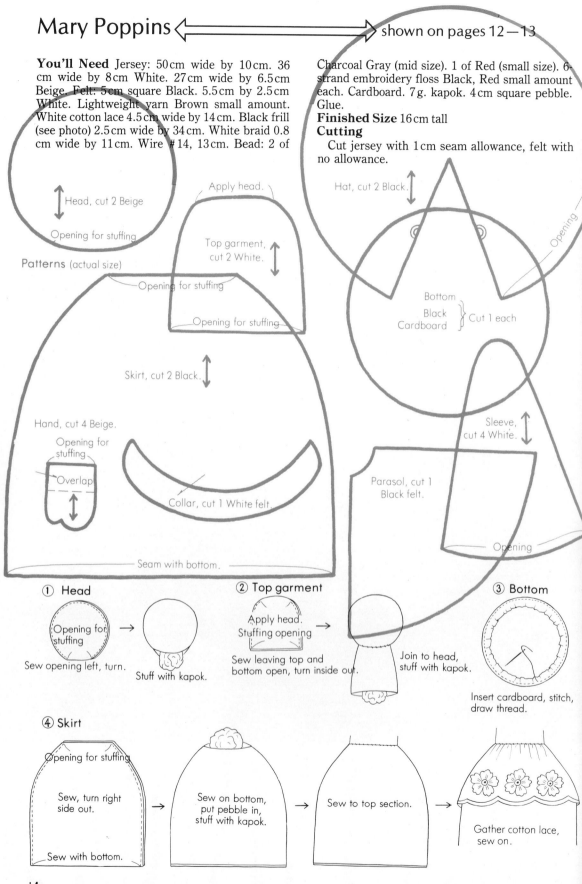

Patterns (actual size)

Head, cut 2 Beige
Opening for stuffing

Apply head.

Top garment, cut 2 White.
Opening for stuffing
Opening for stuffing

Hat, cut 2 Black.

Opening

Bottom
Black
Cardboard } Cut 1 each

Skirt, cut 2 Black.

Sleeve, cut 4 White.

Hand, cut 4 Beige.
Opening for stuffing
Overlap

Collar, cut 1 White felt.

Parasol, cut 1 Black felt.

Opening

Seam with bottom.

① Head
Opening for stuffing
Sew opening left, turn.
Stuff with kapok.

② Top garment
Apply head.
Stuffing opening
Sew leaving top and bottom open, turn inside out.
Join to head, stuff with kapok.

③ Bottom
Insert cardboard, stitch, draw thread.

④ Skirt
Opening for stuffing
Sew, turn right side out.
Sew with bottom.
→
Sew on bottom, put pebble in, stuff with kapok.
→
Sew to top section.
→
Gather cotton lace, sew on.

⑤ Hands ⑥ Sleeves ⑦ Hair (lightweight yarn)

Opening for stuffing

Sew leaving opening, turn.

...ff in kapok, close.

Sew leaving bottom, turn.

Gather bottom side, sew on hand.

Cardboard

18 cm

Wind 24 times around.

5cm   5cm

Fasten.

Sew on where fastened, glue top steady.

⑧ Hat

Sew right sides together.

Sew 2 pieces, right sides together, turn, close opening.

Opening

Sew on back.

Finished Diagram

Sew on Straight stitch with 2 strands in Black.

Charcoal Gray bead

Red bead

Apply rouge.

Sew on.

GLue on.

Straight stitch with 2 strands in Red.

Braid

Sew parasol on back.

⑨ Parasol

1.5cm

10 cm

Wire

1cm

Glue on felt wrapping 4 times around.

Sew steady.

7cm

Wrap 10cm long frill around, secure to felt below.

Sew on frill.

Wooden Horse)

ou'll Need (for each) Jersey Yellow Brown 23
n wide by 15cm. Felt: 8cm by 4cm Yellow. 7cm
3.5cm Red. Scraps of White, Black, Cherry
nk. Lightweight yarn Green small amount. 30
Gold spangle 0.5cm diameter. 30 beads (mid
ze) Gold. Cardboard. Small amount of kapok.
one of 4cm by 3cm. Glue.
nished Size Refer to chart.
utting
Cut jersey with 1cm seam allowance, felt with
allowance.
ssembly
Sew body leaving opening, turn, insert kapok and
one, sew on bottom.
Attach saddle, tail, and mane referring to chart,
ake features on face.

Patterns (actual size)

Body, cut 2
Yellow brown

Opening for stuffing

Bottom
Yellow Brown
Cardboard } Cut 1 each

Ear, cut 4 Yellow Brown

Opening

Saddle
Yellow
Red
cut 1 each

Eye Cut 2 each

Nose, cut 2 Cherry Pink

Black   White

nished diagram, instructions for boy and girl, see page 92.

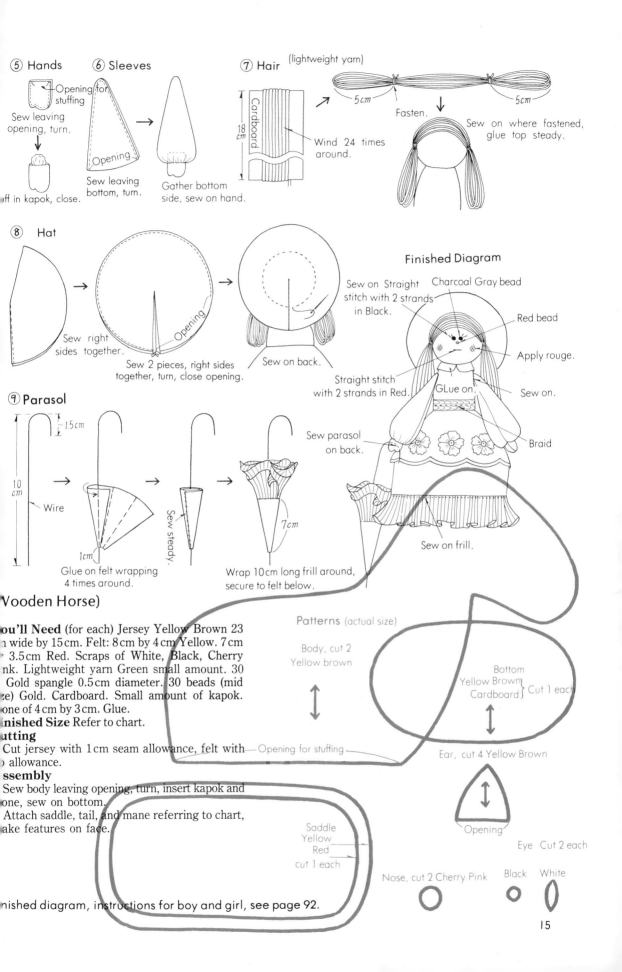

Daddy Long-Legs

Instructions on page 18.

Instructions on page 102.

Daddy Long-Legs ⟵⟶

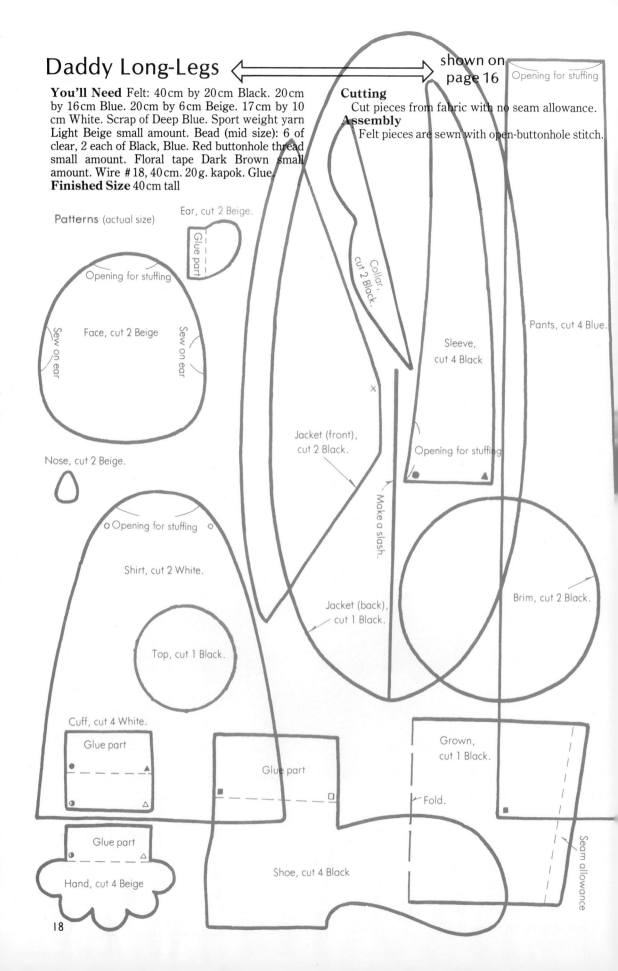

You'll Need Felt: 40 cm by 20 cm Black. 20 cm by 16 cm Blue. 20 cm by 6 cm Beige. 17 cm by 10 cm White. Scrap of Deep Blue. Sport weight yarn Light Beige small amount. Bead (mid size): 6 of clear, 2 each of Black, Blue. Red buttonhole thread small amount. Floral tape Dark Brown small amount. Wire #18, 40 cm. 20 g. kapok. Glue.
Finished Size 40 cm tall

Cutting
  Cut pieces from fabric with no seam allowance.
Assembly
  Felt pieces are sewn with open-buttonhole stitch.

Patterns (actual size)

Ear, cut 2 Beige.

Glue part

Opening for stuffing

Face, cut 2 Beige

Sew on ear

Sew on ear

Nose, cut 2 Beige.

Collar, cut 2 Black.

Sleeve, cut 4 Black

Pants, cut 4 Blue.

Opening for stuffing

Opening for stuffing

Jacket (front), cut 2 Black.

Make a slash.

Opening for stuffing

Shirt, cut 2 White.

Jacket (back), cut 1 Black.

Brim, cut 2 Black.

Top, cut 1 Black.

Cuff, cut 4 White.

Glue part

Grown, cut 1 Black.

Glue part

Fold.

Glue part

Shoe, cut 4 Black

Seam allowance

Hand, cut 4 Beige

18

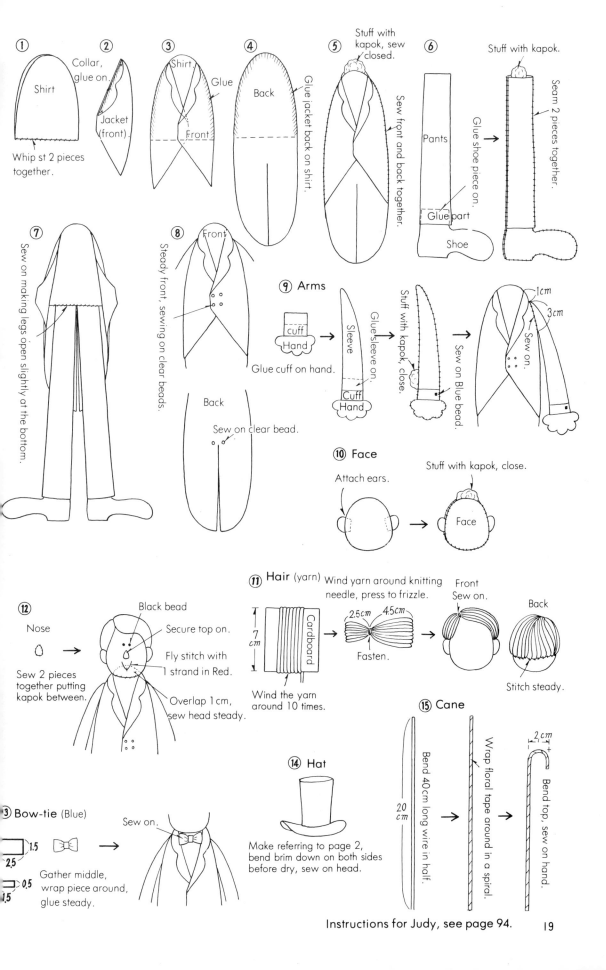

① Shirt
Whip st 2 pieces together.

② Collar, glue on.
Jacket (front).

③ Shirt
Glue
Front

④ Back
Glue jacket back on shirt.

⑤ Stuff with kapok, sew closed.
Sew front and back together.

⑥ Stuff with kapok.
Pants
Glue shoe piece on.
Glue part
Shoe
Seam 2 pieces together.

⑦ Sew on making legs open slightly at the bottom.

⑧ Front
Steady front, sewing on clear beads.
Back
Sew on clear bead.

⑨ Arms
cuff
Hand
Glue cuff on hand.
Glue sleeve on.
Sleeve
Cuff
Hand
Stuff with kapok, close.
Sew on Blue bead.
1cm
3cm
Sew on.

⑩ Face
Attach ears.
Stuff with kapok, close.
Face

⑪ Hair (yarn) Wind yarn around knitting needle, press to frizzle.
7 cm
Cardboard
Wind the yarn around 10 times.
2.5cm 4.5cm
Fasten.
Front
Sew on.
Back
Stitch steady.

⑫ Nose
Sew 2 pieces together putting kapok between.
Black bead
Secure top on.
Fly stitch with 1 strand in Red.
Overlap 1cm, sew head steady.

⑬ Bow-tie (Blue)
1.5
2.5
0.5
1.5
Gather middle, wrap piece around, glue steady.
Sew on.

⑭ Hat
Make referring to page 2, bend brim down on both sides before dry, sew on head.

⑮ Cane
20 cm
Bend 40cm long wire in half.
Wrap floral tape around in a spiral.
2 cm
Bend top, sew on hand.

Instructions for Judy, see page 94.   19

MY DARLING DOLLS

Instructions on page 22.

Instructions on page 9.

Milly

shown on page 20

You'll Need Broadcloth Maroon 85 cm by 35 cm. Striped lawn Beige 68 cm by 25 cm. Sheeting 42 cm by 17 cm. Fine wool Off-White 22 cm by 14.5 cm. Velveteen Brown 32 cm by 12 cm. Felt: 30 cm square Purple. 16 cm by 7 cm Dark Green. Scrap of Dark Brown. Trimming lace Brown 0.8 cm wide by 230 cm. Ribbon tape Beige 0.4 cm wide by 1 m, Deep Red 1.2 cm wide by 60 cm. 6-strand embroidery floss Red, Brown, Green small amount each. 5 g. Beige mohair. Elastic 25 cm long. Chopstick. Small amount of cotton batting. 100 g. kapok.

Finished Size 50 cm tall

Cutting

Cut vest and brim with no seam allowance, felt pieces with 0.5 cm allowance, remaining pieces with 1 cm allowance.

Patterns are on page 82.

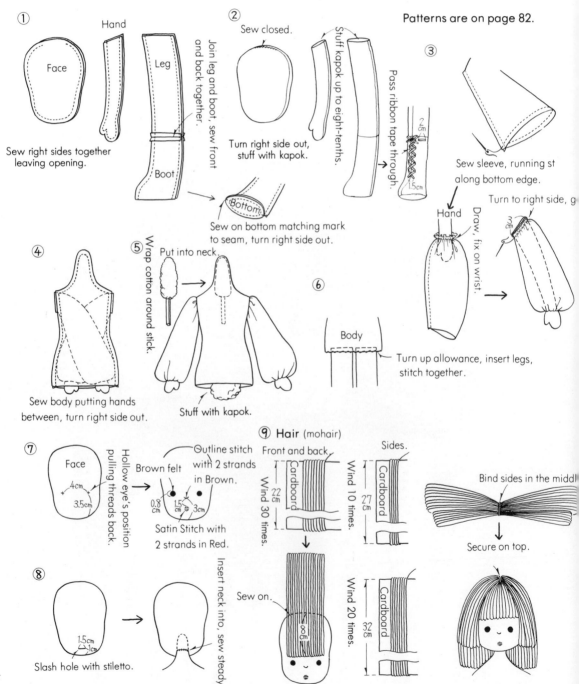

① Face / Hand / Leg / Boot — Sew right sides together leaving opening. Join leg and boot, sew front and back together.

② Sew closed. Turn right side out, stuff with kapok. Stuff kapok up to eight-tenths. Sew on bottom matching mark to seam, turn right side out.

③ Pass ribbon tape through. Sew sleeve, running st along bottom edge. Hand. Draw, fix on wrist. Turn to right side, g

④ Sew body putting hands between, turn right side out.

⑤ Wrap cotton around stick. Put into neck. Stuff with kapok.

⑥ Body — Turn up allowance, insert legs, stitch together.

⑦ Face — Hollow eye's position pulling threads back. Brown felt. Outline stitch with 2 strands in Brown. Satin Stitch with 2 strands in Red. 4cm / 3.5cm / 0.8cm / 1.5cm / 3cm

⑧ Slash hole with stiletto. 1.5cm / 1cm. Insert neck into, sew steady.

⑨ Hair (mohair) — Front and back. Sides. Cardboard. Wind 30 times. 22cm. Wind 10 times. 27cm. Wind 20 times. 32cm. 8cm. Sew on. Bind sides in the middl. Secure on top.

22

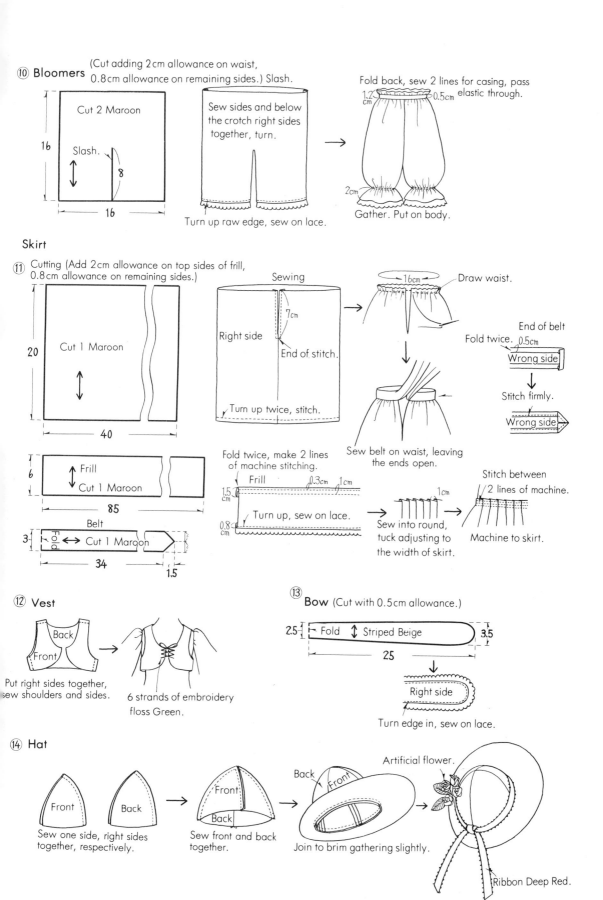

⑩ Bloomers (Cut adding 2cm allowance on waist, 0.8cm allowance on remaining sides.) Slash.

Cut 2 Maroon

Slash.

16

16

8

Sew sides and below the crotch right sides together, turn.

Turn up raw edge, sew on lace.

Fold back, sew 2 lines for casing, pass elastic through.

1.2 cm   0.5cm

2cm

Gather. Put on body.

Skirt

⑪ Cutting (Add 2cm allowance on top sides of frill, 0.8cm allowance on remaining sides.)

Cut 1 Maroon

20

40

Sewing

Right side

7cm

End of stitch.

Turn up twice, stitch.

←16cm→ Draw waist.

Sew belt on waist, leaving the ends open.

End of belt

Fold twice. 0.5cm

Wrong side

Stitch firmly.

Wrong side

6

Frill
Cut 1 Maroon

85

Belt

3   Fold ←→ Cut 1 Maroon

34

1.5

Fold twice, make 2 lines of machine stitching.

Frill   0.3cm   1cm

1.5 cm

Turn up, sew on lace.

0.8 cm

Sew into round, tuck adjusting to the width of skirt.

1cm

Stitch between 2 lines of machine.

Machine to skirt.

⑫ Vest

Back

Front

Put right sides together, sew shoulders and sides.

6 strands of embroidery floss Green.

⑬ Bow (Cut with 0.5cm allowance.)

2.5   Fold ↕ Striped Beige   3.5

25

Right side

Turn edge in, sew on lace.

⑭ Hat

Front   Back

Sew one side, right sides together, respectively.

Front

Back

Sew front and back together.

Back   Front

Join to brim gathering slightly.

Artificial flower.

Ribbon Deep Red.

Instructions on page 26.

Instructions on page 104.

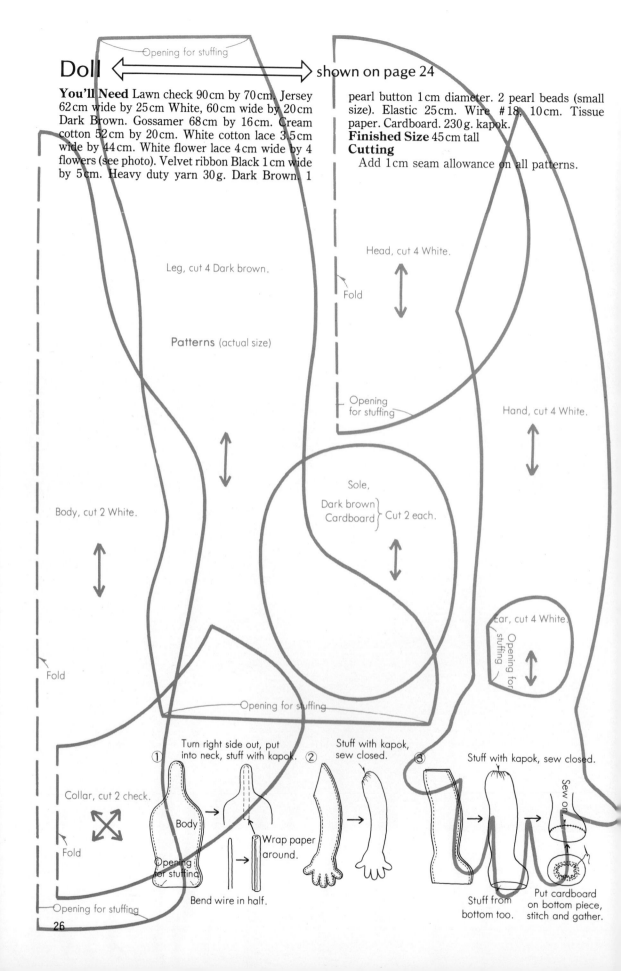

Doll

shown on page 24

You'll Need Lawn check 90cm by 70cm. Jersey 62cm wide by 25cm White, 60cm wide by 20cm Dark Brown. Gossamer 68cm by 16cm. Cream cotton 52cm by 20cm. White cotton lace 3.5cm wide by 44cm. White flower lace 4cm wide by 4 flowers (see photo). Velvet ribbon Black 1cm wide by 5cm. Heavy duty yarn 30g. Dark Brown. 1 pearl button 1cm diameter. 2 pearl beads (small size). Elastic 25cm. Wire #18, 10cm. Tissue paper. Cardboard. 230g. kapok.

Finished Size 45cm tall

Cutting

Add 1cm seam allowance on all patterns.

Opening for stuffing

Leg, cut 4 Dark brown.

Patterns (actual size)

Head, cut 4 White.

Fold

Opening for stuffing

Hand, cut 4 White.

Body, cut 2 White.

Sole,
Dark brown }
Cardboard } Cut 2 each.

Ear, cut 4 White.
Opening for stuffing

Fold

Opening for stuffing

Collar, cut 2 check.

Fold

Opening for stuffing

① Turn right side out, put into neck, stuff with kapok.

Body

Opening for stuffing

Wrap paper around.

Bend wire in half.

② Stuff with kapok, sew closed.

③ Stuff with kapok, sew closed.

Sew on

Stuff from bottom too.

Put cardboard on bottom piece, stitch and gather.

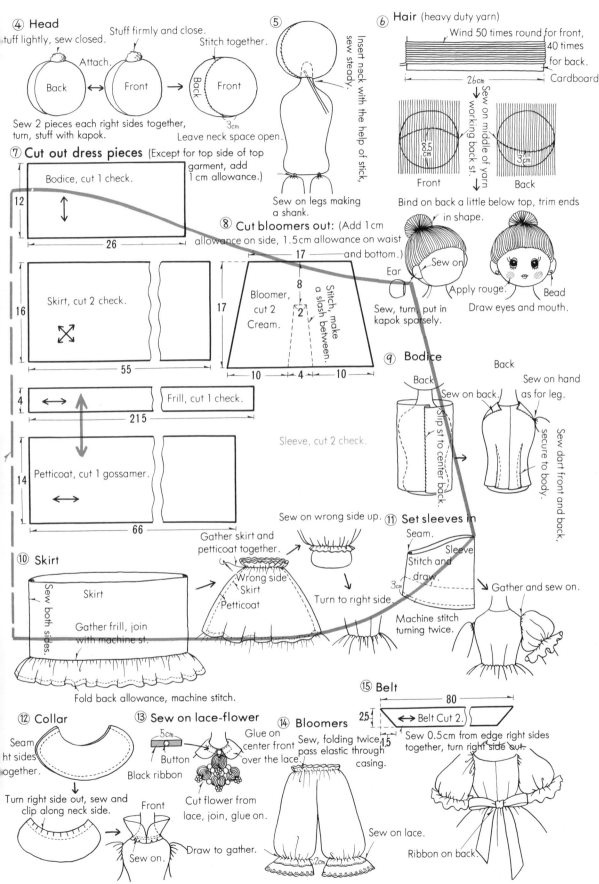

④ **Head**
tuff lightly, sew closed.

Stuff firmly and close.

Attach.

Stitch together.

Back ↔ Front → Back Front

3cm

Sew 2 pieces each right sides together, turn, stuff with kapok.

Leave neck space open.

⑤ Insert neck with the help of stick, sew steady.

Sew on legs making a shank.

⑥ **Hair** (heavy duty yarn)
Wind 50 times round for front, 40 times for back.

26cm — Cardboard

Sew on middle of yarn working back st.

8.5 cm

Front

3cm

Back

Bind on back a little below top, trim ends in shape.

Sew on

Ear

Apply rouge.

Bead

Draw eyes and mouth.

⑦ **Cut out dress pieces** (Except for top side of top garment, add 1 cm allowance.)

Bodice, cut 1 check.

12

26

Skirt, cut 2 check.

16

55

⑧ **Cut bloomers out:** (Add 1 cm allowance on side, 1.5cm allowance on waist and bottom.)

17

Bloomer, cut 2 Cream.

8

2

Stitch, make a slash between.

17

10 4 10

Sew, turn, put in kapok sparsely.

4

215

Frill, cut 1 check.

Sleeve, cut 2 check.

⑨ **Bodice**

Back

Back

Sew on back.

Slip st to center back.

Back

Sew on hand as for leg.

Sew dart front and back, secure to body.

Petticoat, cut 1 gossamer.

14

66

Sew on wrong side up.

⑪ **Set sleeves in**

Seam.

Sleeve

Stitch and draw.

3cm

Gather and sew on.

Gather skirt and petticoat together.

Wrong side Skirt

Petticoat

Turn to right side.

Machine stitch turning twice.

⑩ **Skirt**

Sew both sides.

Skirt

Gather frill, join with machine st.

Fold back allowance, machine stitch.

⑮ **Belt**

80

25

Belt Cut 2.

1.5

Sew 0.5cm from edge right sides together, turn right side out.

⑫ **Collar**

Seam ht sides ogether.

Turn right side out, sew and clip along neck side.

Front

Sew on.

Draw to gather.

⑬ **Sew on lace-flower**

5cm

Button

Black ribbon

Glue on center front over the lace.

Cut flower from lace, join, glue on.

⑭ **Bloomers**

Sew, folding twice pass elastic through casing.

Sew on lace.

2cm

Ribbon on back.

27

PETS
IN THE GREEN FIELD

Instructions on page 30.

Instructions on page 31.

Dog (pair)

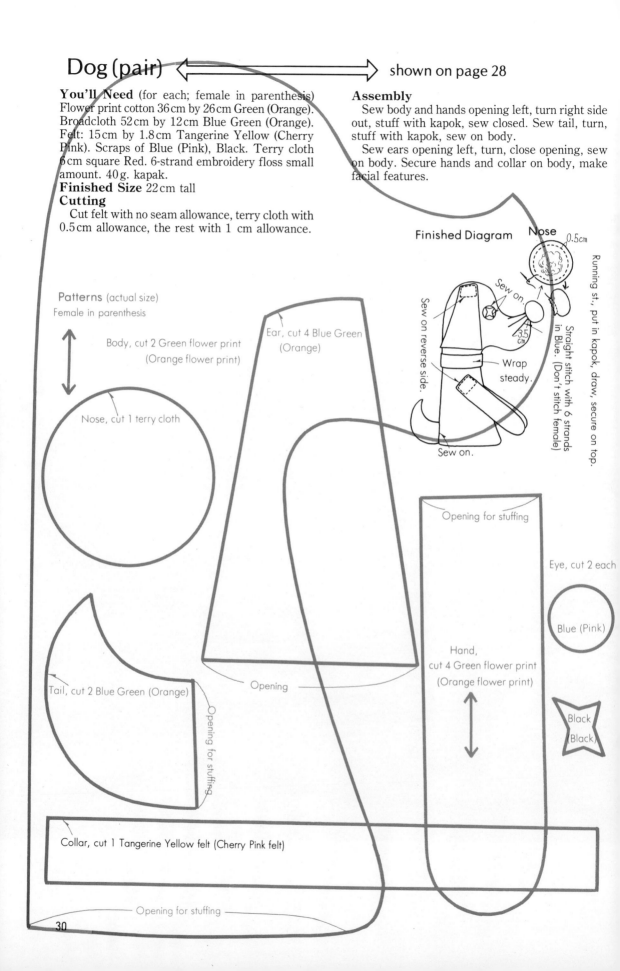

shown on page 28

You'll Need (for each; female in parenthesis)
Flower print cotton 36 cm by 26 cm Green (Orange).
Broadcloth 52 cm by 12 cm Blue Green (Orange).
Felt: 15 cm by 1.8 cm Tangerine Yellow (Cherry Pink). Scraps of Blue (Pink), Black. Terry cloth 6 cm square Red. 6-strand embroidery floss small amount. 40 g. kapak.
Finished Size 22 cm tall
Cutting
Cut felt with no seam allowance, terry cloth with 0.5 cm allowance, the rest with 1 cm allowance.

Assembly
Sew body and hands opening left, turn right side out, stuff with kapok, sew closed. Sew tail, turn, stuff with kapok, sew on body.
Sew ears opening left, turn, close opening, sew on body. Secure hands and collar on body, make facial features.

Finished Diagram   Nose   0.5 cm

Sew on.

Sew on reverse side.

Wrap steady.

3.5 cm

Sew on.

Running st., put in kapok, draw, secure on top.

Straight stitch with 6 strands in Blue. (Don't stitch female)

Patterns (actual size)
Female in parenthesis

Body, cut 2 Green flower print
(Orange flower print)

Ear, cut 4 Blue Green
(Orange)

Nose, cut 1 terry cloth

Opening for stuffing

Eye, cut 2 each

Blue (Pink)

Tail, cut 2 Blue Green (Orange)

Opening

Opening for stuffing

Hand,
cut 4 Green flower print
(Orange flower print)

Black
(Black)

Collar, cut 1 Tangerine Yellow felt (Cherry Pink felt)

Opening for stuffing

Cat & Fox

shown on page 29

Patterns (actual size)

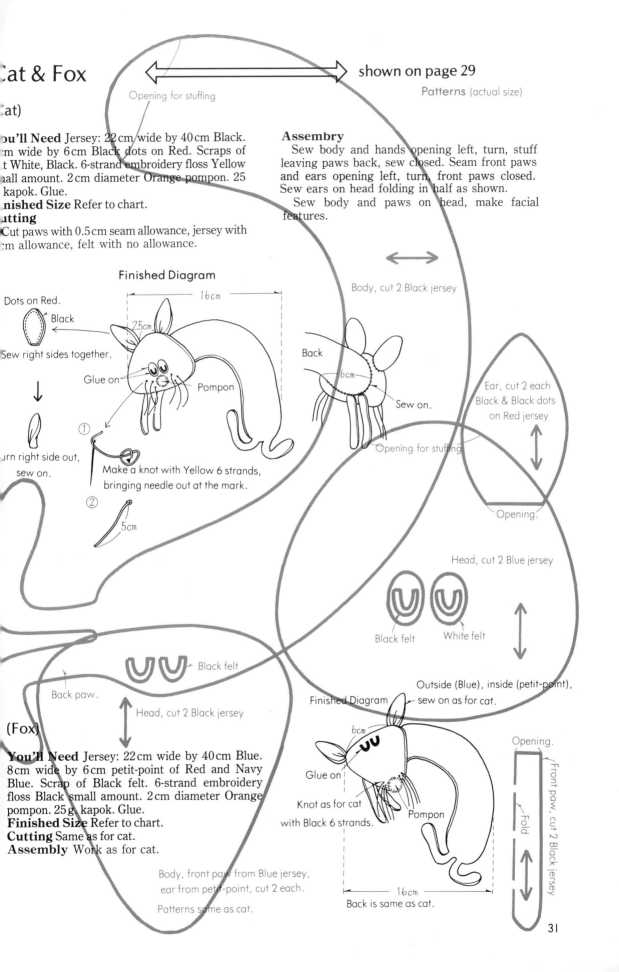

(Cat)

You'll Need Jersey: 22 cm wide by 40 cm Black. cm wide by 6 cm Black dots on Red. Scraps of t White, Black. 6-strand embroidery floss Yellow all amount. 2 cm diameter Orange pompon. 25 kapok. Glue.

Finished Size Refer to chart.

Cutting
Cut paws with 0.5 cm seam allowance, jersey with cm allowance, felt with no allowance.

Assembry

Sew body and hands opening left, turn, stuff leaving paws back, sew closed. Seam front paws and ears opening left, turn, front paws closed. Sew ears on head folding in half as shown.

Sew body and paws on head, make facial features.

Opening for stuffing

Finished Diagram

Dots on Red.

Black

Sew right sides together.

16 cm

2.5 cm

Glue on

Pompon

Turn right side out, sew on.

① Make a knot with Yellow 6 strands, bringing needle out at the mark.

②

5 cm

Body, cut 2 Black jersey

Back

6 cm

Sew on.

Opening for stuffing

Ear, cut 2 each Black & Black dots on Red jersey

Opening.

Head, cut 2 Blue jersey

Black felt   White felt

Outside (Blue), inside (petit-point), sew on as for cat.

Black felt

Back paw.

Head, cut 2 Black jersey

Finished Diagram

6 cm

Glue on

Knot as for cat with Black 6 strands.

Pompon

16 cm

Back is same as cat.

Opening.

Front paw, cut 2 Black jersey

Fold

(Fox)

You'll Need Jersey: 22 cm wide by 40 cm Blue. 8 cm wide by 6 cm petit-point of Red and Navy Blue. Scrap of Black felt. 6-strand embroidery floss Black small amount. 2 cm diameter Orange pompon. 25 g. kapok. Glue.

Finished Size Refer to chart.

Cutting Same as for cat.

Assembly Work as for cat.

Body, front paw from Blue jersey, ear from petit-point, cut 2 each.

Patterns same as cat.

Instructions on page 34.

Instructions on page 34.

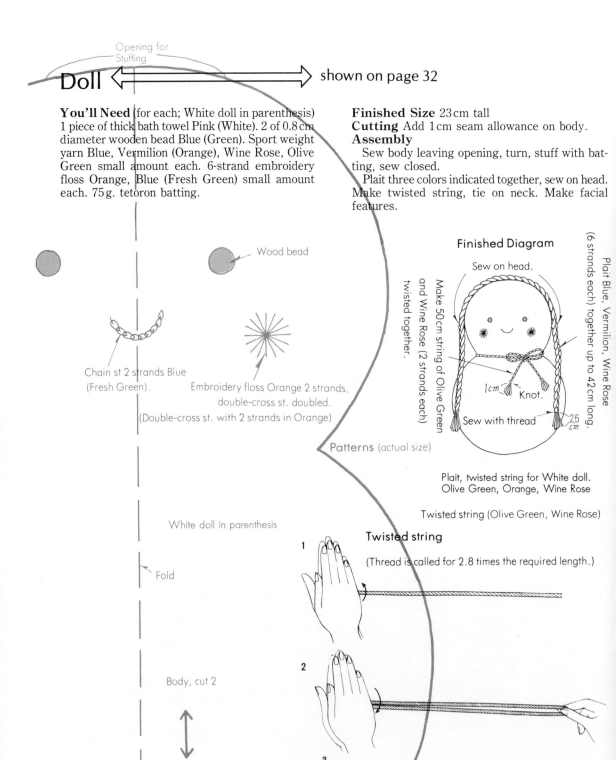

Doll ⟵⟶ shown on page 32

shown on page 32

You'll Need (for each; White doll in parenthesis)
1 piece of thick bath towel Pink (White). 2 of 0.8 cm
diameter wooden bead Blue (Green). Sport weight
yarn Blue, Vermilion (Orange), Wine Rose, Olive
Green small amount each. 6-strand embroidery
floss Orange, Blue (Fresh Green) small amount
each. 75 g. tetoron batting.

Finished Size 23 cm tall
Cutting Add 1 cm seam allowance on body.
Assembly
Sew body leaving opening, turn, stuff with bat-
ting, sew closed.
Plait three colors indicated together, sew on head.
Make twisted string, tie on neck. Make facial
features.

Opening for
Stuffing

Wood bead

Chain st 2 strands Blue
(Fresh Green).

Embroidery floss Orange 2 strands,
double-cross st. doubled.

(Double-cross st. with 2 strands in Orange)

Patterns (actual size)

Make 50 cm string of Olive Green
and Wine Rose (2 strands each)
twisted together.

Plait Blue, Vermilion, Wine Rose
(6 strands each) together up to 42 cm long.

Finished Diagram

Sew on head.

1 cm   Knot.

Sew with thread   2.5 cm

Plait, twisted string for White doll.
Olive Green, Orange, Wine Rose

Twisted string (Olive Green, Wine Rose)

Twisted string

(Thread is called for 2.8 times the required length.)

White doll in parenthesis

Fold

Body, cut 2

1

2

3

Doll ⟵⟶ shown on page 33

shown on page 33

(Boy)

You'll Need Sheeting 36 cm by 24 cm. Striped
jersey 24 cm wide by 8 cm. Soft denim 22 cm by
4.5 cm Blue. Small amount of Brown raffia. 6-
strand embroidery floss Blue, Salmon Pink, Soft

Pink small amount each. 50 g. kapok. Glue.
Finished Size 22 cm tall
Cutting Add 1 cm seam allowance on body.

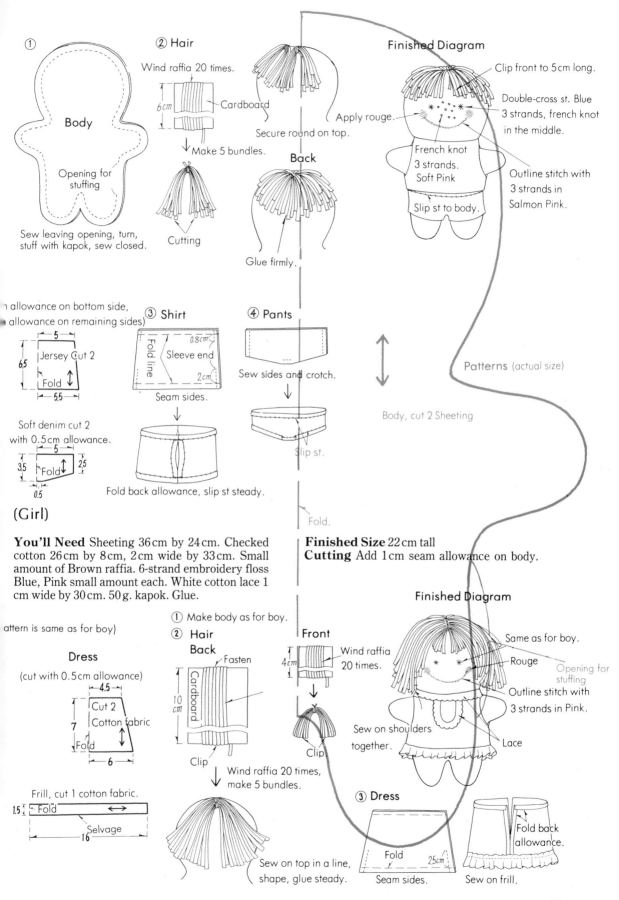

①

Body

Opening for stuffing

Sew leaving opening, turn, stuff with kapok, sew closed.

② Hair

Wind raffia 20 times.

6cm — Cardboard

Secure round on top.

→ Make 5 bundles.

Cutting

Back

Glue firmly.

Finished Diagram

Clip front to 5cm long.

Apply rouge.

Double-cross st. Blue 3 strands, french knot in the middle.

French knot 3 strands. Soft Pink

Outline stitch with 3 strands in Salmon Pink.

Slip st to body.

n allowance on bottom side, allowance on remaining sides)

③ Shirt

Fold line

Sleeve end

0.8cm

2cm

Seam sides.

Fold back allowance, slip st steady.

5
6,5
Jersey Cut 2
Fold
5,5

Soft denim cut 2 with 0.5cm allowance.
5
3,5 Fold 2,5
0,5

④ Pants

Sew sides and crotch.

Slip st.

Patterns (actual size)

Body, cut 2 Sheeting

Fold.

(Girl)

You'll Need Sheeting 36cm by 24cm. Checked cotton 26cm by 8cm, 2cm wide by 33cm. Small amount of Brown raffia. 6-strand embroidery floss Blue, Pink small amount each. White cotton lace 1 cm wide by 30cm. 50g. kapok. Glue.

attern is same as for boy)

Dress

(cut with 0.5cm allowance)
4.5
7 Cut 2 Cotton fabric
Fold
6

Frill, cut 1 cotton fabric.
1,5 Fold ←→
Selvage
16

Finished Size 22cm tall
Cutting Add 1cm seam allowance on body.

① Make body as for boy.

② Hair
Back

Fasten

10 cm Cardboard

Clip

Wind raffia 20 times, make 5 bundles.

Sew on top in a line, shape, glue steady.

Front

4cm

Wind raffia 20 times.

Clip

Finished Diagram

Same as for boy.

Rouge

Opening for stuffing

Outline stitch with 3 strands in Pink.

Lace

Sew on shoulders together.

③ Dress

Fold 25cm

Seam sides.

Fold back allowance.

Sew on frill.

35

Instructions on page 38.

Instructions on page 84.

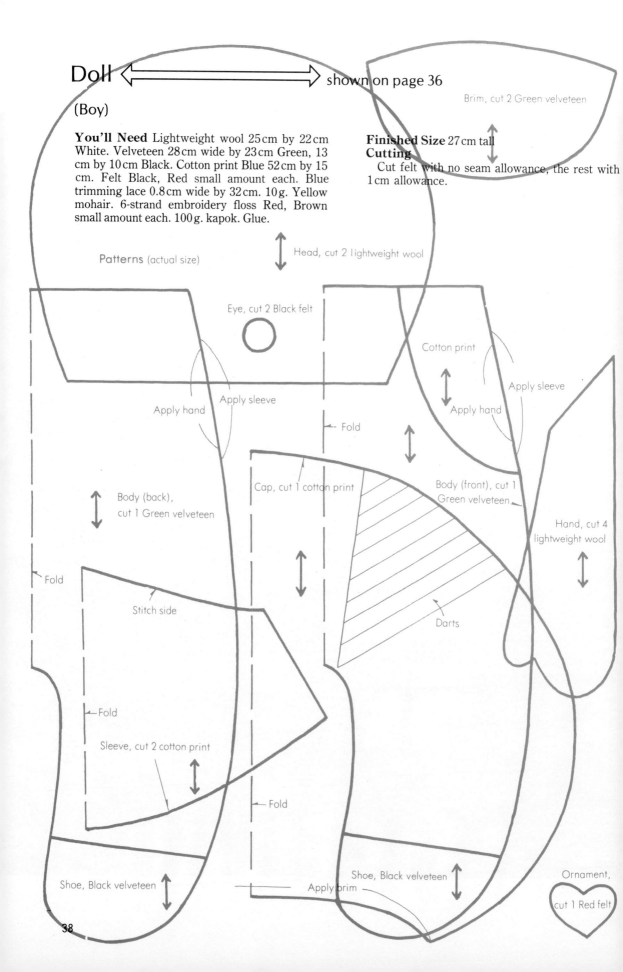

Doll ⟵⟶ shown on page 36

(Boy)

You'll Need Lightweight wool 25 cm by 22 cm White. Velveteen 28 cm wide by 23 cm Green, 13 cm by 10 cm Black. Cotton print Blue 52 cm by 15 cm. Felt Black, Red small amount each. Blue trimming lace 0.8 cm wide by 32 cm. 10 g. Yellow mohair. 6-strand embroidery floss Red, Brown small amount each. 100 g. kapok. Glue.

Finished Size 27 cm tall
Cutting
  Cut felt with no seam allowance, the rest with 1 cm allowance.

Patterns (actual size)

Brim, cut 2 Green velveteen

Head, cut 2 lightweight wool

Eye, cut 2 Black felt

Cotton print

Apply sleeve

Apply hand

Apply sleeve

Apply hand

Fold

Cap, cut 1 cotton print

Body (front), cut 1 Green velveteen

Body (back), cut 1 Green velveteen

Hand, cut 4 lightweight wool

Fold

Stitch side

Darts

Fold

Sleeve, cut 2 cotton print

Fold

Shoe, Black velveteen

Shoe, Black velveteen

Apply brim

Ornament, cut 1 Red felt

38

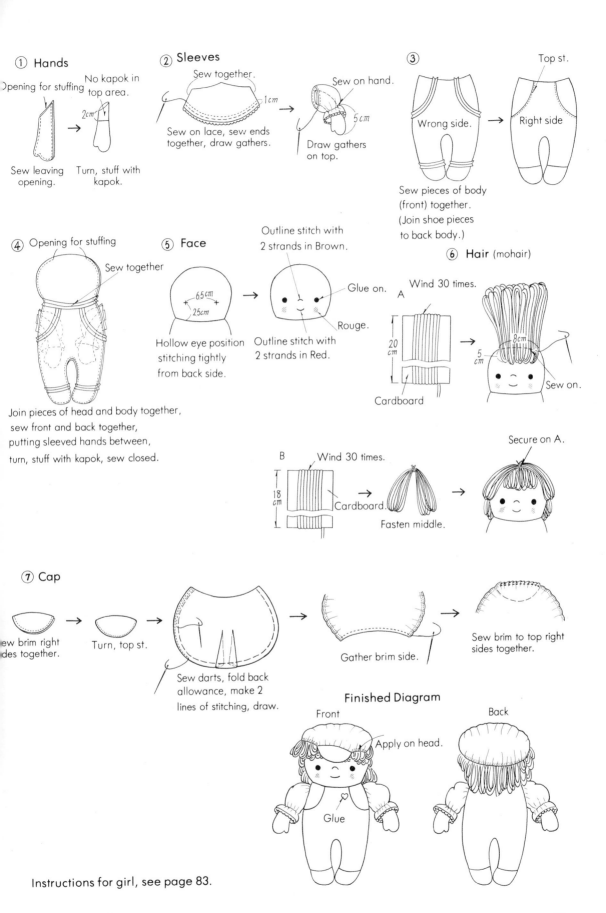

① Hands

Opening for stuffing   No kapok in top area.

2cm

Sew leaving opening.   Turn, stuff with kapok.

② Sleeves

Sew together.

1cm

Sew on lace, sew ends together, draw gathers.

Sew on hand.

5cm

Draw gathers on top.

③

Top st.

Wrong side.   Right side

Sew pieces of body (front) together. (Join shoe pieces to back body.)

④ Opening for stuffing

Sew together

Join pieces of head and body together, sew front and back together, putting sleeved hands between, turn, stuff with kapok, sew closed.

⑤ Face

Outline stitch with 2 strands in Brown.

6.5cm
2.5cm

Glue on.

Rouge.

Hollow eye position stitching tightly from back side.   Outline stitch with 2 strands in Red.

⑥ Hair (mohair)

A   Wind 30 times.

20cm

Cardboard

8cm
5cm

Sew on.

B   Wind 30 times.

18cm

Cardboard.

Fasten middle.

Secure on A.

⑦ Cap

Sew brim right sides together.   Turn, top st.

Sew darts, fold back allowance, make 2 lines of stitching, draw.

Gather brim side.

Sew brim to top right sides together.

Finished Diagram

Front   Back

Apply on head.

Glue

Instructions for girl, see page 83.

Instructions on page 42.

Instructions on page 86.

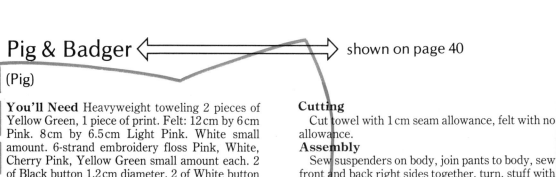

(Pig)

You'll Need Heavyweight toweling 2 pieces of Yellow Green, 1 piece of print. Felt: 12 cm by 6 cm Pink. 8 cm by 6.5 cm Light Pink. White small amount. 6-strand embroidery floss Pink, White, Cherry Pink, Yellow Green small amount each. 2 of Black button 1.2 cm diameter. 2 of White button 1 cm diameter. 74 g. kapok.
Finished Size 25 cm tall

Cutting
Cut towel with 1 cm seam allowance, felt with no allowance.
Assembly
Sew suspenders on body, join pants to body, sew front and back right sides together, turn, stuff with kapok, close opening.
Make facial features referring to chart.

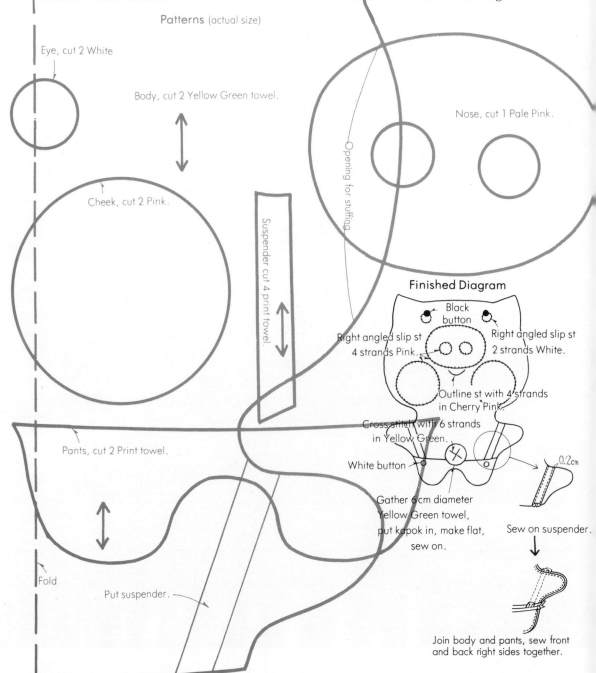

Patterns (actual size)

Eye, cut 2 White

Body, cut 2 Yellow Green towel.

Nose, cut 1 Pale Pink.

Cheek, cut 2 Pink.

Opening for stuffing.

Suspender, cut 4 print towel.

Finished Diagram

Black button

Right angled slip st 4 strands Pink.

Right angled slip st 2 strands White.

Outline st with 4 strands in Cherry Pink.

Cross stitch with 6 strands in Yellow Green.

White button

Pants, cut 2 Print towel.

0.2 cm

Gather 6 cm diameter Yellow Green towel, put kapok in, make flat, sew on.

Sew on suspender.

Fold

Put suspender.

Join body and pants, sew front and back right sides together.

(Badger)

You'll Need Heavyweight hand towel 2 pieces of Orange, small amount of White. Velvet 17cm by 14cm Brown stripe. Felt: 11.5cm by 7.5cm Dark Brown. 11cm by 5.5cm Pink. White small amount. 6-strand embroidery floss Pink, Dark Brown, White, Yellow Green, Red, Orange small amount each. 2 of Black button 1.2cm diameter. 2 of White button 1cm diameter. 75g. kapok. Felt-tip pen Green.

Finished Size 25cm tall
Cutting
   Cut towel and velvet with 1cm seam allowance, felt with no allowance.
Assembly
   Work as for pig.

Patterns (actual size)

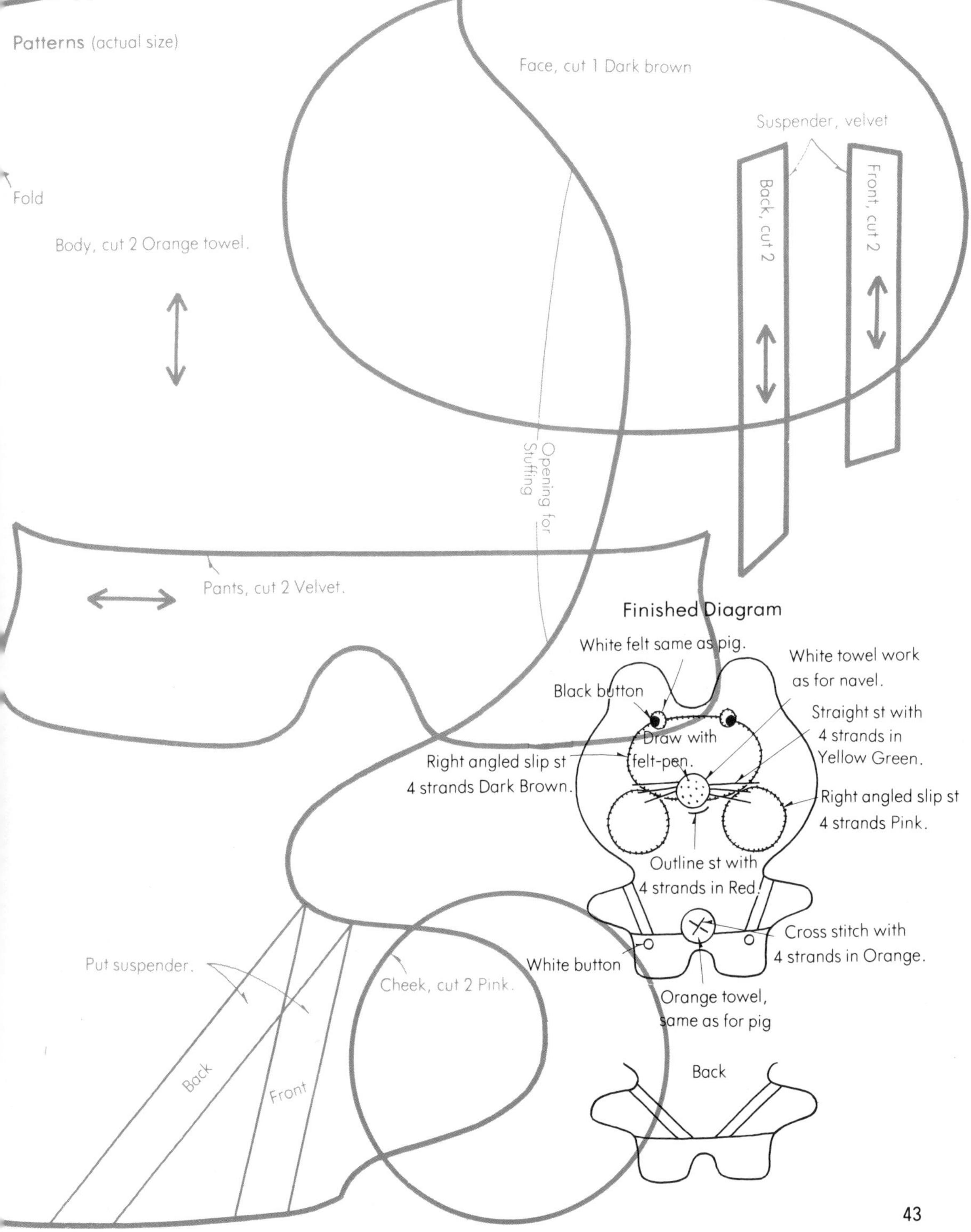

Fold

Body, cut 2 Orange towel.

Face, cut 1 Dark brown

Suspender, velvet

Back, cut 2

Front, cut 2

Opening for Stuffing

Pants, cut 2 Velvet.

Finished Diagram

White felt same as pig.

Black button

Draw with felt-pen.

Right angled slip st 4 strands Dark Brown.

White towel work as for navel.

Straight st with 4 strands in Yellow Green.

Right angled slip st 4 strands Pink.

Outline st with 4 strands in Red.

Cross stitch with 4 strands in Orange.

White button

Orange towel, same as for pig.

Put suspender.

Back

Front

Cheek, cut 2 Pink.

Back

Instructions on page 46.

Instructions on page 107.

Doll (pair)

(Boy)

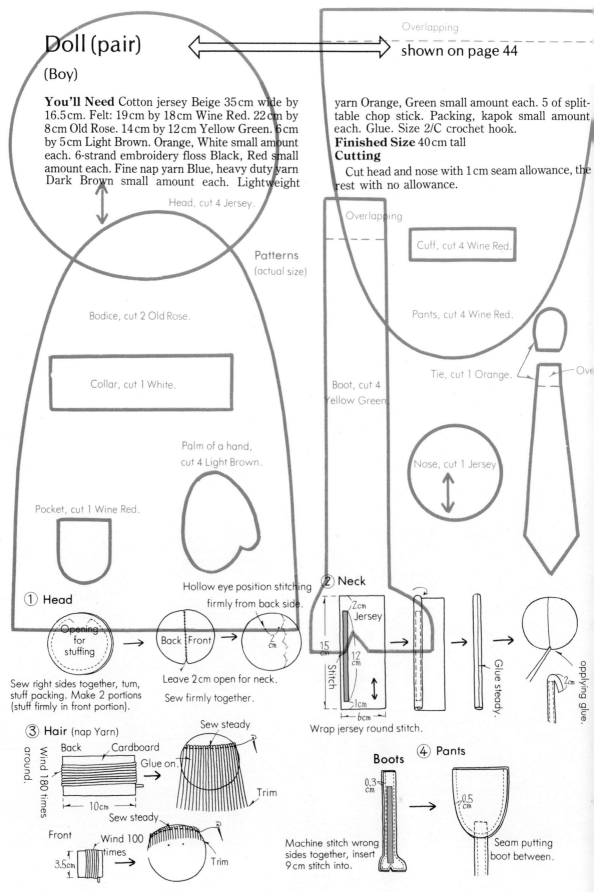

shown on page 44

You'll Need Cotton jersey Beige 35cm wide by 16.5cm. Felt: 19cm by 18cm Wine Red. 22cm by 8cm Old Rose. 14cm by 12cm Yellow Green. 6cm by 5cm Light Brown. Orange, White small amount each. 6-strand embroidery floss Black, Red small amount each. Fine nap yarn Blue, heavy duty yarn Dark Brown small amount each. Lightweight yarn Orange, Green small amount each. 5 of splittable chop stick. Packing, kapok small amount each. Glue. Size 2/C crochet hook.

Finished Size 40 cm tall

Cutting

Cut head and nose with 1 cm seam allowance, the rest with no allowance.

Overlapping

Head, cut 4 Jersey.

Patterns
(actual size)

Overlapping

Cuff, cut 4 Wine Red.

Bodice, cut 2 Old Rose.

Pants, cut 4 Wine Red.

Collar, cut 1 White.

Boot, cut 4 Yellow Green.

Tie, cut 1 Orange.

Ove

Palm of a hand, cut 4 Light Brown.

Nose, cut 1 Jersey

Pocket, cut 1 Wine Red.

Hollow eye position stitching firmly from back side.

① Head

Opening for stuffing

Back Front

2 cm

Sew right sides together, turn, stuff packing. Make 2 portions (stuff firmly in front portion).

Leave 2 cm open for neck.

Sew firmly together.

② Neck

2cm Jersey

15 cm

Stitch

12 cm

1cm

bcm

Wrap jersey round stitch.

Glue steady.

applying glue.

2cm

③ Hair (nap Yarn)

Wind 180 times around.

Back

Cardboard

Glue on.

10cm

Sew steady

Sew steady

Trim

Front

Wind 100 times

3.5cm

Trim

④ Pants

Boots

0.3 cm

Machine stitch wrong sides together, insert 9 cm stitch into.

0.5 cm

Seam putting boot between.

46

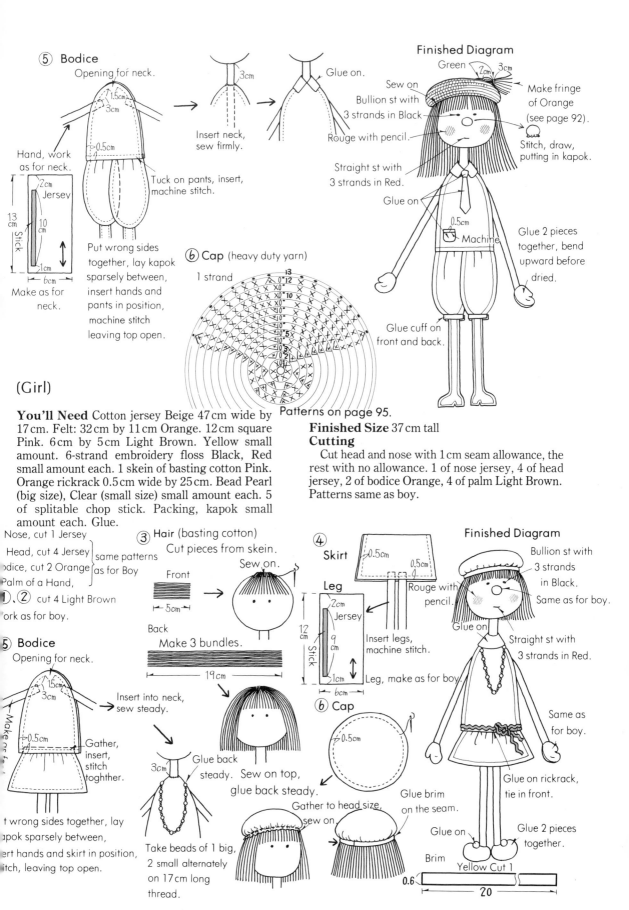

⑤ **Bodice**

Opening for neck.

1.5cm
3cm

Hand, work as for neck.

0.5cm

13cm Stick
2cm Jersey
10cm
1cm
6cm

Make as for neck.

Tuck on pants, insert, machine stitch.

Insert neck, sew firmly.

Glue on.

Put wrong sides together, lay kapok sparsely between, insert hands and pants in position, machine stitch leaving top open.

⑥ **Cap** (heavy duty yarn)

1 strand

13
0 12
X0 10
X0
X0 10
5
3
0
13

Finished Diagram

Green 2cm 3cm

Sew on
Bullion st with
3 strands in Black

Make fringe of Orange (see page 92).

Stitch, draw, putting in kapok

Rouge with pencil.

Straight st with 3 strands in Red.

Glue on

0.5cm
Machine

Glue 2 pieces together, bend upward before dried.

Glue cuff on front and back.

(Girl)

You'll Need Cotton jersey Beige 47 cm wide by 17 cm. Felt: 32 cm by 11 cm Orange. 12 cm square Pink. 6 cm by 5 cm Light Brown. Yellow small amount. 6-strand embroidery floss Black, Red small amount each. 1 skein of basting cotton Pink. Orange rickrack 0.5 cm wide by 25 cm. Bead Pearl (big size), Clear (small size) small amount each. 5 of splitable chop stick. Packing, kapok small amount each. Glue.

Patterns on page 95.

Finished Size 37 cm tall
Cutting

Cut head and nose with 1 cm seam allowance, the rest with no allowance. 1 of nose jersey, 4 of head jersey, 2 of bodice Orange, 4 of palm Light Brown. Patterns same as boy.

Nose, cut 1 Jersey
Head, cut 4 Jersey
Bodice, cut 2 Orange
Palm of a Hand,
①.② cut 4 Light Brown
Work as for boy.

same patterns as for Boy

③ **Hair** (basting cotton)

Cut pieces from skein.

Sew on.

Front
5cm

Back
Make 3 bundles.

19cm

Insert into neck, sew steady.

3cm
Glue back steady. Sew on top, glue back steady.

Take beads of 1 big, 2 small alternately on 17cm long thread.

⑤ **Bodice**

Opening for neck.

1.5cm
3cm

0.5cm

Make as for

Gather, insert, stitch toghther.

t wrong sides together, lay apok sparsely between, ert hands and skirt in position, itch, leaving top open.

④ **Skirt**

0.5cm 0.5cm

Leg

2cm Jersey
12cm Stick
9cm
1cm
6cm

Insert legs, machine stitch.

Leg, make as for boy.

⑥ **Cap**

0.5cm

Glue brim on the seam.

Gather to head size, sew on.

Glue on

Brim

Finished Diagram

Bullion st with 3 strands in Black. Same as for boy.

Rouge with pencil.

Glue on

Straight st with 3 strands in Red.

Same as for boy.

Glue on rickrack, tie in front.

Glue on

Glue 2 pieces together.

Yellow Cut 1
0.6
20

DELIGHTFUL FELLOWS

Instructions on page 50.

Out Bathing — Indian — Bride — Novice — In the Snow

shown on pages 48—49

You'll Need (for each) (2 Black beads mid size, cardboard, small amount of kapok, glue) Indian) Felt: 11 cm by 4 cm Beige. 8 cm by 4.5 cm Rust. 9 cm by 3.5 cm Moss Green. 10 cm by 1 cm Mustard. Small amount of Yellow Green. 6-strand embroidery floss Dark Brown, Orange, Gold Brown small amount each. Lightweight yarn Dark Brown small amount. Wire #24 small amount. Felt-tip pen Green. Bride) Felt: 13 cm by 4 cm Light Pink. 9 cm by 3 cm Deep Pink. 9 cm by 3.5 cm White. 6-strand embroidery floss Pink small amount. Sport weight yarn Ivory small amount. Nylon mesh 25 cm by 6 cm White. 12 beads (mid size) White. Out Bathing) Felt: 22 cm by 4 cm Light Pink. Deep Pink small amount. Terry cloth 25 cm by 4 cm Deep Pink. 6-strand embroidery floss Pink, ring-yarn Brown small amount each. In the Snow) Felt: 13 cm by 6 cm Brown. 11 cm by 4 cm Light Pink. 9 cm by 3.5 cm Mustard. Red, Orange small amount each. 6-strand embroidery floss Red, Gold Brown, Orange small amount each. Lightweight yarn Dark Brown small amount. Novice) Felt: 14 cm by 4 cm White. 12 cm by 4 cm Beige. 20 cm by 1.5 cm Blue. 5.5 cm by 3.5 cm Pale Blue. 6-strand embroidery floss Red, lightweight yarn Yellow small amount each. 1 bead (mid size) Red. Toothpick.

Finished Size 7 cm tall.

Cutting Cut each piece with no seam allowance.

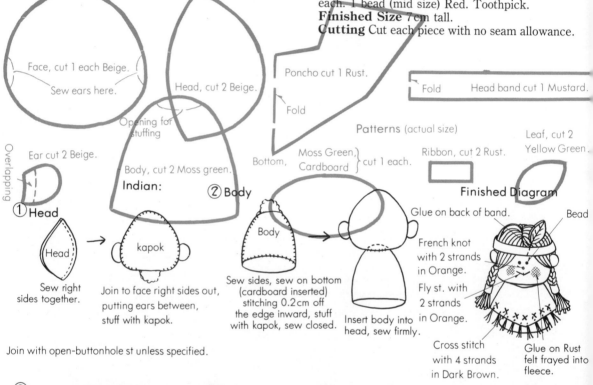

Face, cut 1 each Beige.
Sew ears here.

Head, cut 2 Beige.

Poncho cut 1 Rust.

Fold

Fold   Head band cut 1 Mustard.

Opening for stuffing

Overlapping

Ear cut 2 Beige.

Body, cut 2 Moss green.

Bottom, Moss Green, Cardboard } cut 1 each.

Patterns (actual size)

Ribbon, cut 2 Rust.

Leaf, cut 2 Yellow Green.

Indian:

① Head

Head

Sew right sides together.

Join to face right sides out, putting ears between, stuff with kapok.

② Body

Body

kapok

Sew sides, sew on bottom (cardboard inserted) stitching 0.2 cm off the edge inward, stuff with kapok, sew closed.

Insert body into head, sew firmly.

Glue on back of band.

French knot with 2 strands in Orange.

Fly st. with 2 strands in Orange.

Cross stitch with 4 strands in Dark Brown.

Finished Diagram

Bead

Glue on Rust felt frayed into fleece.

Join with open-buttonhole st unless specified.

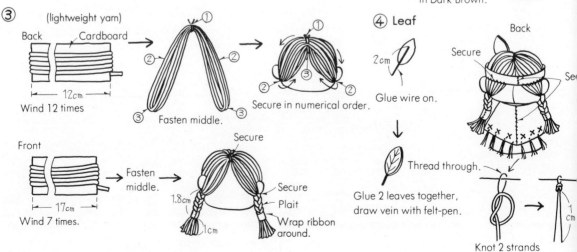

③ (lightweight yarn)

Back   Cardboard

├— 12 cm —┤
Wind 12 times

Fasten middle.

Secure in numerical order.

Front

├— 17 cm —┤
Wind 7 times.

Fasten middle.

Secure
Plait
1.8 cm
1 cm
Wrap ribbon around.

④ Leaf

2 cm

Glue wire on.

Thread through.

Glue 2 leaves together, draw vein with felt-pen.

Back

Secure

Knot 2 strands Gold Brown together.

Bride:

2 of ear Light Pink,
1 of face Light Pink,
2 of head Light Pink,
2 of body White.
Bottom of White,
cardboard 1 each.
} Patterns same as Indian.

①.②
Work as for Indian.

③ **Hair**(Wind yarn around
knitting needle, press to frizzle.)

Cardboard

Wind frizzle
around 8 times.
↓Fasten middle.
20cm

Secure on top, sew 6 strands
each straightened on both sides,
secure back straightening down
to ears.

Patterns (actual size)

6
1.5
Gather.
Veil nylon mesh cut 1.
25

Hand,
cut 2 Light Pink

Flower,
cut 12 Deep Pink.

Finished Diagram

Gather veil, sew on head.
French knot with
2 strands in Pink.
Secure with bead
(apply 3 pieces in front).
Sew on bead.
Glue on felt
Deep Pink frayed
into fleece.
Secure
Couching st
with 2 strands
in Pink
Secure
Secure center with bead.

Out Bathing

2 of head, 1 of face, 2 of ear,
2 of body Light Pink.
of Light Pink, Cardboard 1 each.
nd Light Pink same pattern as bride.

Towel, cut 1 terry cloth.
2.5
8

Turban cut 1 terry cloth.
0.7
17

} Patterns same
as Indian.

①.②
Work as
for Indian.

③ **Hair** (ring-yarn)

Cardboard

9cm
Wind 20 times.

3cm
Wind 10 times.
Fasten middle, sew on top.

Glue on felt Deep
Pink frayed
into fleece.

Secure

Back Secure

Finished Diagram

Make a knot,
sew on.
Bead.
French knot
with 2 strands
in Pink
Couching st
with 2 strands
in Pink.
Sew steady.
Wrap towel over,
glue steady.

In the Snow:

of head, 1 of face, 2 of ear Light Pink.
of body Mustard.
ttom 1 each of Mustard, cardboard.
} Patterns same as Indian.

①.②
Work as for Indian.

4
Fold
Hood
cut 1 Brown.
6.5
2.5
6

Belt, cut 1 Red.
0.9
7

③ (lightweight yarn)

Cardboard

10cm
Wind 30 times.

Secure on top,
trim front,
glue steady.

④

Seam with
open-buttonhole st.
Belt,
glue steady.
2cm
Straight st with
2 strands in Red.

Finished Diagram

Glue on Orange felt
frayed into fleecy state.

Couching st
with 2 strands
in Orange.

Clip along.

Straight st with
6 strands in
Gold Brown.
Bead
French knot with
2 strands in Orange.
Secure

Back

Secure to body.

Instructions for Novice, see page 93.

Instructions on page 54.

Instructions on page 55.

Stray Animals ⟵⟶ shown on page 52

(Monkey)

You'll Need Jersey Brown 32cm wide by 6cm.
Felt Pink, Red, White, Black small amount each.
Pearl cotton floss Red, 6-strand embroidery floss
Pink small amount each. 10g. kapok. Glue.
Finished Size 8cm tall
Cutting Cut jersey with 0.5cm seam allowance,
felt with no allowance.
Assembly
  Sew head and body opening left, turn, stuff with
kapok, sew closed. Sew body on head, tucking
allowance along the opening.
  Make features referring to chart, apply identification tag.

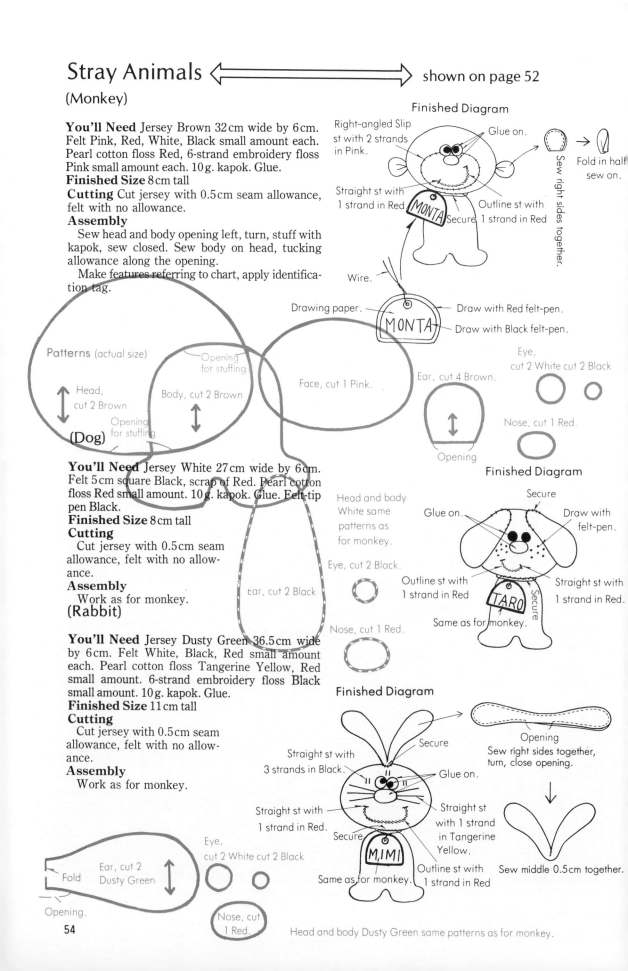

Finished Diagram

Right-angled Slip st with 2 strands in Pink.

Glue on.

Sew right sides together.

Fold in half sew on.

Straight st with 1 strand in Red

MONTA

Outline st with Secure 1 strand in Red

Wire.

Drawing paper.

MONTA

Draw with Red felt-pen.

Draw with Black felt-pen.

Eye, cut 2 White cut 2 Black

Ear, cut 4 Brown.

Nose, cut 1 Red.

Patterns (actual size)

Head, cut 2 Brown

Opening for stuffing

Body, cut 2 Brown

Opening for stuffing

Face, cut 1 Pink.

Opening

Finished Diagram

(Dog)

You'll Need Jersey White 27cm wide by 6cm.
Felt 5cm square Black, scrap of Red. Pearl cotton
floss Red small amount. 10g. kapok. Glue. Felt-tip
pen Black.
Finished Size 8cm tall
Cutting
  Cut jersey with 0.5cm seam
allowance, felt with no allowance.
Assembly
  Work as for monkey.

(Rabbit)

You'll Need Jersey Dusty Green 36.5cm wide
by 6cm. Felt White, Black, Red small amount
each. Pearl cotton floss Tangerine Yellow, Red
small amount. 6-strand embroidery floss Black
small amount. 10g. kapok. Glue.
Finished Size 11cm tall
Cutting
  Cut jersey with 0.5cm seam
allowance, felt with no allowance.
Assembly
  Work as for monkey.

Head and body White same patterns as for monkey.

Eye, cut 2 Black.

Ear, cut 2 Black

Nose, cut 1 Red.

Secure

Glue on.

Draw with felt-pen.

Outline st with 1 strand in Red

TARO

Straight st with 1 strand in Red.

Same as for monkey.

Finished Diagram

Straight st with 3 strands in Black.

Secure

Opening

Sew right sides together, turn, close opening.

Glue on.

Straight st with 1 strand in Red.

Straight st with 1 strand in Tangerine Yellow.

Secure

MIMI

Outline st with 1 strand in Red

Same as for monkey.

Sew middle 0.5cm together.

Ear, cut 2 Dusty Green

Fold

Opening.

Eye, cut 2 White cut 2 Black

Nose, cut 1 Red.

Head and body Dusty Green same patterns as for monkey.

54

Pets on the Train

shown on page 53

(Dog)

Patterns (actual size)

You'll Need Jersey Light Brown 21 cm wide by 11 cm. Terry cloth Tangerine Yellow, White felt small amount each. 1.5 cm diameter Brown pompon. 2 Black buttons 0.7 cm diameter. White sewing cotton. 10 g. kapok. Felt-tip pen Navy Blue.
Finished Size 10 cm tall
Cutting
  Cut felt with no seam allowance, the rest with 0.5 cm allowance. For jersey reverse side is used.
Assembly
  Sew body leaving opening, turn, stuff with kapok, sew closed.
  Make features referring to chart.

(Monkey)

You'll Need Jersey Green 23 cm wide by 10 cm. Felt Light Beige, Orange, White, Black small amount each. 6-strand embroidery floss Vermilion small amount. 10 g. kapok. Glue.
Finished Size 8.5 cm tall
Cutting
  Cut jersey with 0.5 cm seam allowance, felt with no allowance.
Assembly Work as for dog.

(Rabbit)

You'll Need Jersey Blue 21 cm wide by 15 cm. Felt Brown, White, Cherry Pink small amount each. 6-strand embroidery floss Orange small amount. 10 g. kapok. Glue.
Finished Size 13.5 cm tall
Cutting
  Cut jersey with 0.5 cm seam allowance, felt with no allowance.
Making Instructions Work as for dog.

Instructions for pig and rat, see page 85.

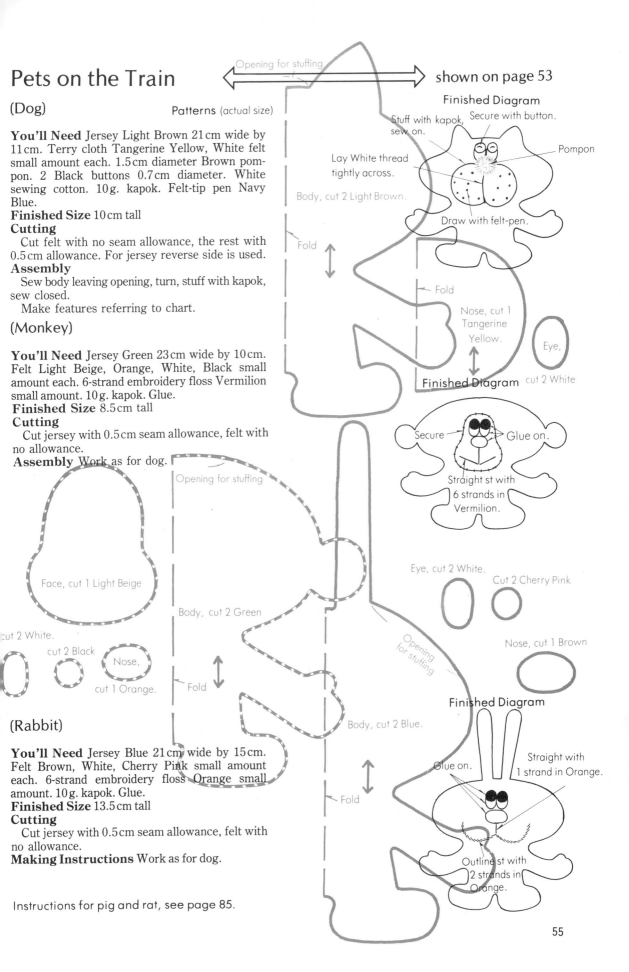

Opening for stuffing

Finished Diagram
Stuff with kapok, sew on.
Secure with button.
Pompon
Lay White thread tightly across.
Body, cut 2 Light Brown.
Draw with felt-pen.
Fold

Fold
Nose, cut 1 Tangerine Yellow.
Eye, cut 2 White
Finished Diagram

Secure
Glue on.
Straight st with 6 strands in Vermilion.

Opening for stuffing

Face, cut 1 Light Beige

Body, cut 2 Green

cut 2 White
cut 2 Black
Nose, cut 1 Orange.
Fold

Eye, cut 2 White.
Cut 2 Cherry Pink
Nose, cut 1 Brown

Opening for stuffing

Body, cut 2 Blue.

Fold

Finished Diagram
Glue on.
Straight with 1 strand in Orange.
Outline st with 2 strands in Orange.

Nymphs

Instructions on page 58.

Instructions on page 59.

Nymphs ⟵=====⟹ shown on page 56

You'll Need (for all) Nylon mesh stocking, small amount of cotton batting, tissue paper, 2 cm long bamboo stick, scrap of Dark Brown georgette, 6-strand embroidery floss Pink small amount, glue. A) Braid 2.5 cm wide by 23 cm (see photo). 1 skein of 6-strand embroidery floss Cream. Beige felt small amount. B) Braid 2.5 cm wide by 23 cm (see photo). 0.4 cm wide embroidery ribbon Pink 1/2 skein, Dusty Green small amount. Heavy-weight ribbon Yellow Green 0.3 cm wide by 12 cm. 1 skein of 6-strand embroidery floss Light Yellow Brown. Felt Light Pink small amount. C) Striped tyrolean braid

1.5 cm wide by 10 cm. 1 skein of 6-strand embroidery floss Light Brown. Small amount of Beige felt. D) Checked tyrolean braid 1.8 cm by 10 cm. 1 skein of 6-strand embroidery floss Blue. Felt Vermilion small amount. E) Floral tyrolean braid 1.8 cm by 10 cm. 1 skein of 6-strand embroidery floss Magenta. Felt 10.5 cm by 6.5 cm Fresh Green, Light Pink small amount.

Finished Size Refer to chart.
Cutting Cut each piece with no seam allowance.

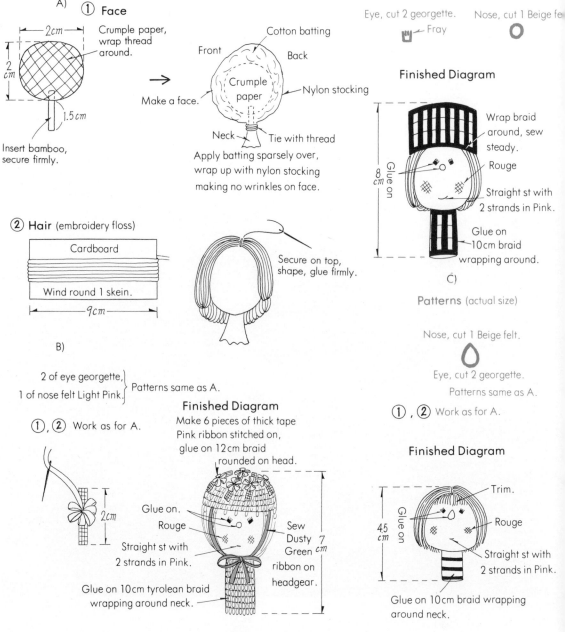

Patterns (actual size)

Eye, cut 2 georgette.   Nose, cut 1 Beige fe[lt]

←Fray

A) ① Face

2 cm — 2 cm

Crumple paper, wrap thread around.

1.5 cm

Insert bamboo, secure firmly.

Make a face. →

Front   Cotton batting   Back

Crumple paper — Nylon stocking

Neck — Tie with thread

Apply batting sparsely over, wrap up with nylon stocking making no wrinkles on face.

② Hair (embroidery floss)

Cardboard

Wind round 1 skein.

9 cm

Secure on top, shape, glue firmly.

Finished Diagram

8 cm — Glue on

Wrap braid around, sew steady.

Rouge

Straight st with 2 strands in Pink.

Glue on 10 cm braid wrapping around.

C)
Patterns (actual size)

Nose, cut 1 Beige felt.

Eye, cut 2 georgette.

Patterns same as A.

①, ② Work as for A.

B)

2 of eye georgette, 1 of nose felt Light Pink.⟩ Patterns same as A.

①, ② Work as for A.

2 cm

Finished Diagram

Make 6 pieces of thick tape Pink ribbon stitched on, glue on 12 cm braid rounded on head.

Glue on.
Rouge

Straight st with 2 strands in Pink.

Sew Dusty Green ribbon on headgear. 7 cm

Glue on 10 cm tyrolean braid wrapping around neck.

Finished Diagram

4.5 cm — Glue on

Trim.
Rouge

Straight st with 2 strands in Pink.

Glue on 10 cm braid wrapping around neck.

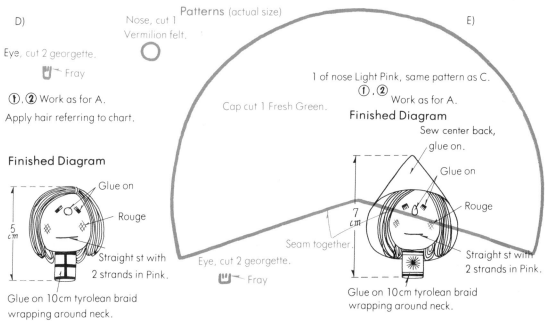

D)

Patterns (actual size)

Nose, cut 1
Vermilion felt.

Eye, cut 2 georgette.
🔲 ← Fray

①, ② Work as for A.

Apply hair referring to chart.

E)

1 of nose Light Pink, same pattern as C.

①, ② Work as for A.

Finished Diagram

Sew center back,
glue on.

Glue on

Rouge

7 cm

Seam together.

Straight st with
2 strands in Pink.

Glue on 10cm tyrolean braid
wrapping around neck.

Finished Diagram

Glue on

Rouge

5 cm

Straight st with
2 strands in Pink.

Glue on 10cm tyrolean braid
wrapping around neck.

Eye, cut 2 georgette.
🔲 ← Fray

Singing in Chorus ⟵⟶ shown on page 57

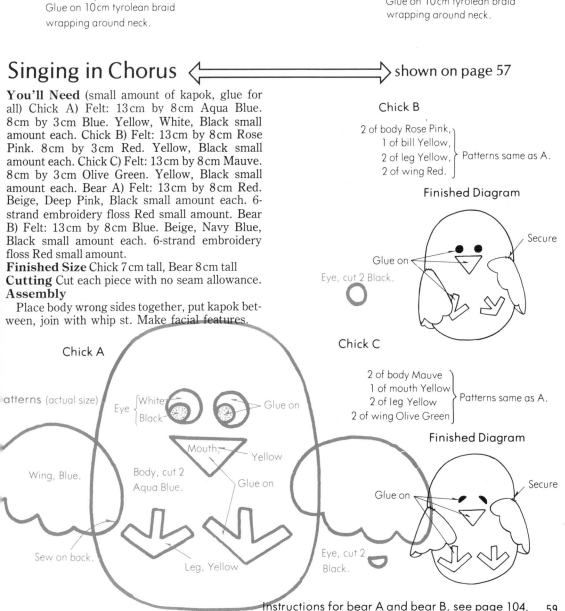

You'll Need (small amount of kapok, glue for all) Chick A) Felt: 13cm by 8cm Aqua Blue. 8cm by 3cm Blue. Yellow, White, Black small amount each. Chick B) Felt: 13cm by 8cm Rose Pink. 8cm by 3cm Red. Yellow, Black small amount each. Chick C) Felt: 13cm by 8cm Mauve. 8cm by 3cm Olive Green. Yellow, Black small amount each. Bear A) Felt: 13cm by 8cm Red. Beige, Deep Pink, Black small amount each. 6-strand embroidery floss Red small amount. Bear B) Felt: 13cm by 8cm Blue. Beige, Navy Blue, Black small amount each. 6-strand embroidery floss Red small amount.

Finished Size Chick 7cm tall, Bear 8cm tall

Cutting Cut each piece with no seam allowance.

Assembly

Place body wrong sides together, put kapok between, join with whip st. Make facial features.

Chick A

Patterns (actual size)

Eye { White / Black

Glue on

Mouth, Yellow

Glue on

Wing, Blue.

Body, cut 2
Aqua Blue.

Sew on back.

Leg, Yellow

Chick B

2 of body Rose Pink,
1 of bill Yellow,
2 of leg Yellow,
2 of wing Red.
} Patterns same as A.

Finished Diagram

Secure

Glue on

Eye, cut 2 Black.

Chick C

2 of body Mauve
1 of mouth Yellow
2 of leg Yellow
2 of wing Olive Green
} Patterns same as A.

Finished Diagram

Secure

Glue on

Eye, cut 2
Black.

Instructions for bear A and bear B, see page 104.   59

Playing Cards

Intructions on page 62.

Instructions on page 62.

Playing Cards ⟵⟶ shown on page 60

You'll Need Bear) Felt: 10 cm by 7 cm Blue. White, Navy Blue small amount each. 6-strand embroidery floss Orange, Charcoal Gray, White, Blue small amount each. 1.5 cm diameter Blue pompon. 1 cm diameter Black button. Small amount of kapok. Rabbit) Felt: 10 cm by 7 cm Deep Pink. White jersey small amount. 6-strand embroidery floss Charcoal Gray, Brown, Red small amount each. 1.5 cm diameter Light Pink pompon. 0.4 cm long wooden bead Purple. Small amount of kapok. Cat) Felt: 10 cm by 7 cm Cream. White, Brown small amount each. 6-strand embroidery floss Charcoal Gray, Brown, Orange, White small amount each. 1 cm diameter Brown button. Small amount of kapok.

Finished Size Refer to chart.

Cutting

Cut felt with no seam allowance, jersey with 1 cm allowance.

Assembly

Put 2 pieces right sides out, put kapok between, join with open-buttonhole st. Make facial features.

Patterns (actual size)

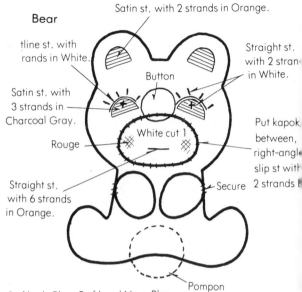

Bear

Satin st. with 2 strands in Orange.

tline st. with rands in White.

Straight st. with 2 stran in White.

Button

Satin st. with 3 strands in Charcoal Gray.

Put kapok between, right-angle slip st with

White cut 1

Rouge

Secure 2 strands

Straight st. with 6 strands in Orange.

Pompon

2 of body Blue, 2 of hand Navy Blue.

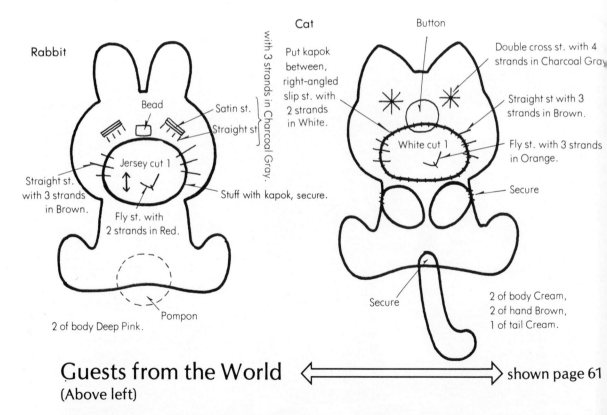

Rabbit

Bead

Satin st.

Straight st

Jersey cut 1

Straight st. with 3 strands in Brown.

Fly st. with 2 strands in Red.

Pompon

2 of body Deep Pink.

with 3 strands in Charcoal Gray.

Cat

Put kapok between, right-angled slip st. with 2 strands in White.

Stuff with kapok, secure.

Button

Double cross st. with 4 strands in Charcoal Gray

Straight st with 3 strands in Brown.

White cut 1

Fly st. with 3 strands in Orange.

Secure

Secure

2 of body Cream, 2 of hand Brown, 1 of tail Cream.

Guests from the World ⟵⟶ shown page 61
(Above left)

You'll Need Felt: 10 cm by 5 cm Blue. 9 cm by 5 cm Light Beige. Lightweight yarn 7 g. Yellow. 6-strand embroidery floss Green, Tangerine Yellow, Red, White small amount each. Ribbon 1.7 cm wide by 1 m. Spangle: 2 of star-shape 1 cm diameter Pink, 3 of flower-shape 1.3 cm diameter Pearl. 5 g. kapok.

Finished Size 12 cm tall

Cutting Cut each piece with no seam allowance.

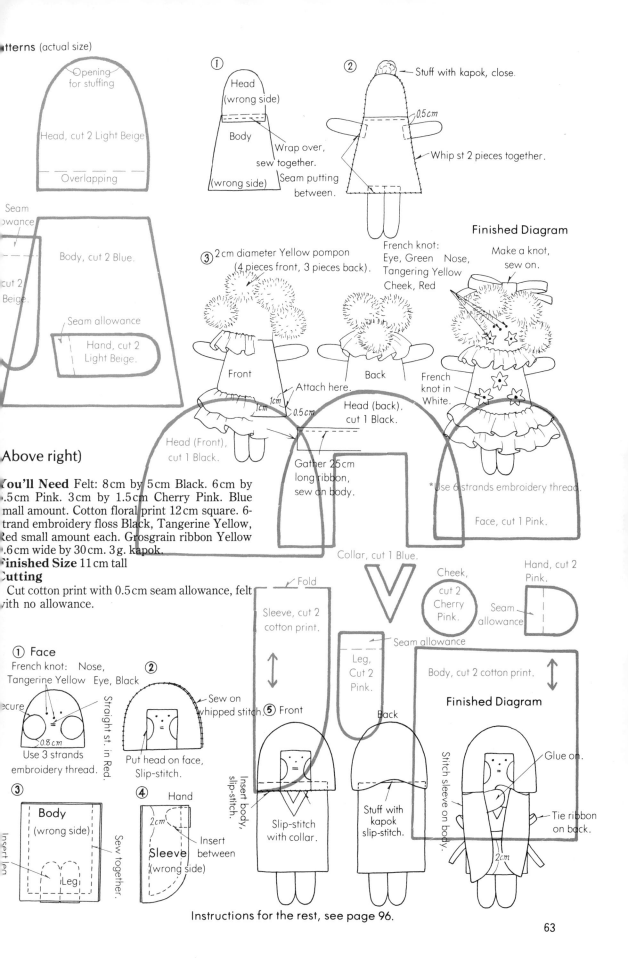

Patterns (actual size)

Opening for stuffing

Head, cut 2 Light Beige

Overlapping

Seam allowance

Body, cut 2 Blue.

cut 2 Beige.

Seam allowance

Hand, cut 2 Light Beige.

① Head (wrong side)

Body (wrong side)

Wrap over, sew together.

Seam putting between.

② Stuff with kapok, close.

0.5 cm

Whip st 2 pieces together.

Finished Diagram

③ 2 cm diameter Yellow pompon (4 pieces front, 3 pieces back).

Front   Back

French knot:
Eye, Green   Nose, Tangering Yellow
Cheek, Red

Make a knot, sew on.

French knot in White.

1 cm   1 cm   0.5 cm

Attach here.

Head (Front), cut 1 Black.

Head (back), cut 1 Black.

Gather 25 cm long ribbon, sew on body.

* Use 6 strands embroidery thread.

Face, cut 1 Pink.

(Above right)

You'll Need Felt: 8 cm by 5 cm Black. 6 cm by 5.5 cm Pink. 3 cm by 1.5 cm Cherry Pink. Blue small amount. Cotton floral print 12 cm square. 6-strand embroidery floss Black, Tangerine Yellow, Red small amount each. Grosgrain ribbon Yellow 0.6 cm wide by 30 cm. 3 g. kapok.
Finished Size 11 cm tall
Cutting Cut cotton print with 0.5 cm seam allowance, felt with no allowance.

Fold

Sleeve, cut 2 cotton print.

Collar, cut 1 Blue.

Cheek, cut 2 Cherry Pink.

Hand, cut 2 Pink.

Seam allowance

Leg, Cut 2 Pink.

Seam allowance

Body, cut 2 cotton print.

Finished Diagram

① **Face**
French knot: Nose, Tangerine Yellow   Eye, Black

Secure

0.8 cm

Use 3 strands embroidery thread.

Straight st. in Red.

② Sew on whipped stitch.

Put head on face, Slip-stitch.

⑤ Front   Back

Insert body, slip-stitch.

Slip-stitch with collar.

Stuff with kapok slip-stitch.

③ Body (wrong side)

Insert leg

Leg

Sew together.

④ Hand

2 cm

Insert between

Sleeve (wrong side)

Stitch sleeve on body.

Glue on.

Tie ribbon on back.

2 cm

Instructions for the rest, see page 96.

63

HOLIDAY IN ANIMAL LAND

Instructions on page 87.

Rabbit & Monkey

Pillow (pair)

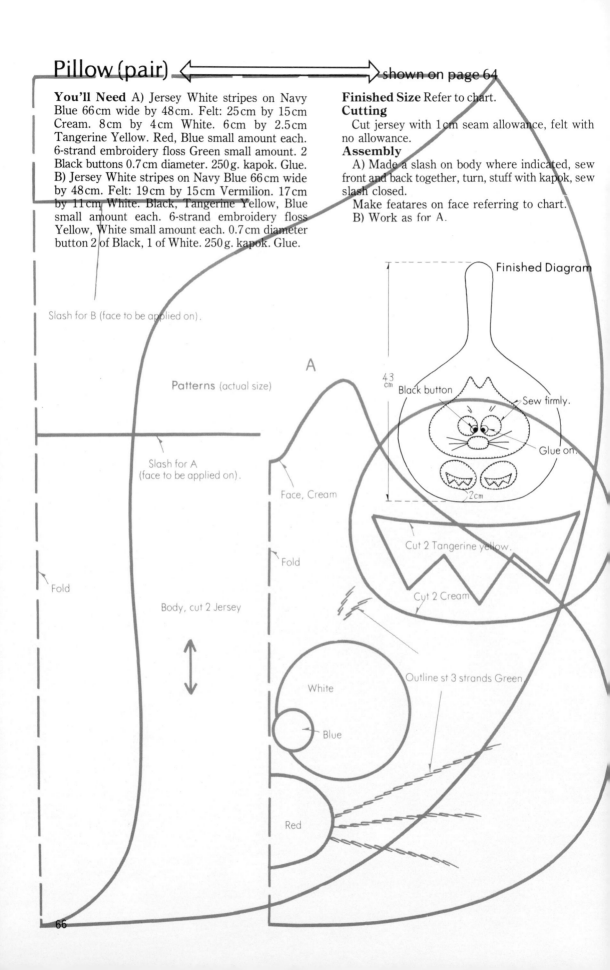

shown on page 64

You'll Need A) Jersey White stripes on Navy Blue 66cm wide by 48cm. Felt: 25cm by 15cm Cream. 8cm by 4cm White. 6cm by 2.5cm Tangerine Yellow. Red, Blue small amount each. 6-strand embroidery floss Green small amount. 2 Black buttons 0.7cm diameter. 250g. kapok. Glue.
B) Jersey White stripes on Navy Blue 66cm wide by 48cm. Felt: 19cm by 15cm Vermilion. 17cm by 11cm White. Black, Tangerine Yellow, Blue small amount each. 6-strand embroidery floss Yellow, White small amount each. 0.7cm diameter button 2 of Black, 1 of White. 250g. kapok. Glue.

Finished Size Refer to chart.
Cutting
　Cut jersey with 1cm seam allowance, felt with no allowance.
Assembly
　A) Made a slash on body where indicated, sew front and back together, turn, stuff with kapok, sew slash closed.
　Make featares on face referring to chart.
　B) Work as for A.

Slash for B (face to be applied on).

Finished Diagram

Patterns (actual size)

A

Slash for A
(face to be applied on).

Face, Cream

Fold

Fold

Body, cut 2 Jersey

White

Blue

Red

43 cm

Black button

Sew firmly.

Glue on.

2cm

Cut 2 Tangerine yellow.

Cut 2 Cream

Outline st 3 strands Green

66

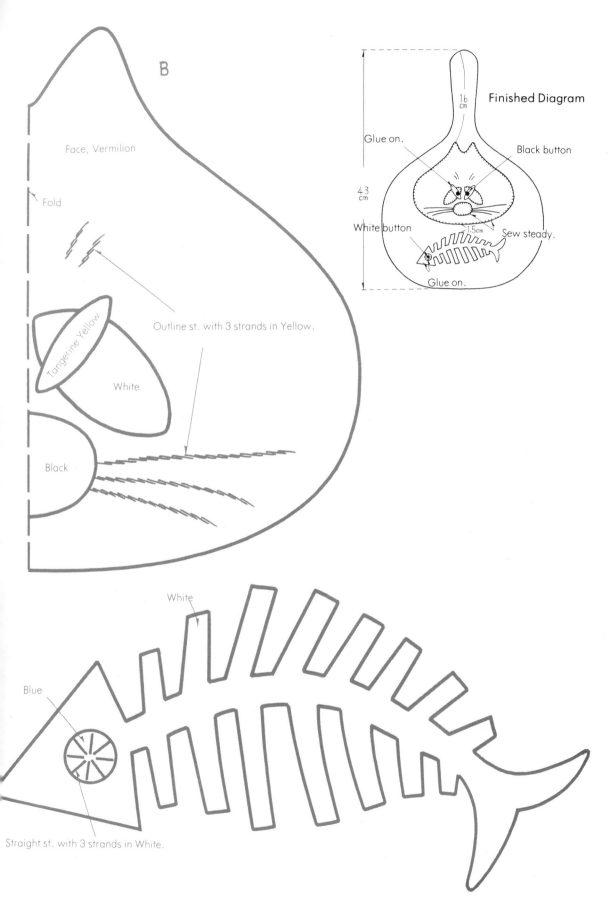

B

Face, Vermilion

Fold

Outline st. with 3 strands in Yellow.

Tangerine Yellow

White

Black

Finished Diagram

16 cm

43 cm

Glue on.

Black button

White button

Sew steady.

1.5cm

Glue on.

White

Blue

Straight st. with 3 strands in White.

67

⇧

Mother Donkey & Her Baby

Instructions on page 70.

Instructions on page 88.

Giraffe & Zebra

Mother Donkey & Her Baby

⟵⟶ shown on page 68

(Mother)

You'll Need Jersey 45cm wide by 25cm, 10cm square White. Felt: 6cm square Cherry Pink. 5cm by 4cm Yellow Green. 6cm by 3cm each of Rouge, Deep Pink. 4cm by 2cm Tangerine Yellow. Black, White small amount each. Lightweight yarn 15g. Yellow. 6-strand embroidery floss Red, Black small amount each. 55g. kapok. Glue. Crochet hook size 2/C.

Finished Size Refer to chart.

Cutting
  Cut jersey with 0.5cm seam allowance, felt with no allowance.

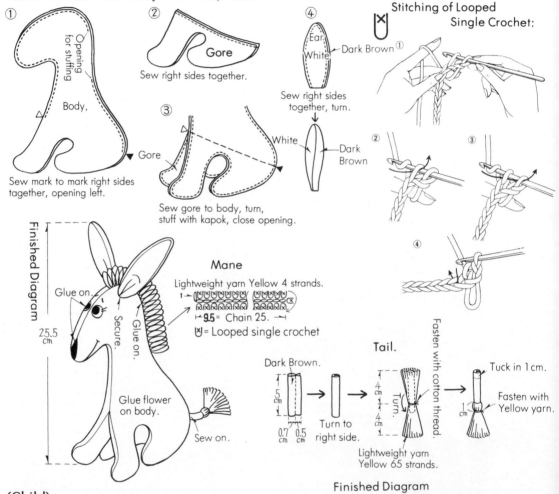

① Opening for stuffing. Body,

Sew mark to mark right sides together, opening left.

② Gore. Sew right sides together.

③ Gore. Sew gore to body, turn, stuff with kapok, close opening.

④ Ear White ← Dark Brown ① Sew right sides together, turn. White — Dark Brown

Stitching of Looped Single Crochet: ① ② ③ ④

Finished Diagram

Glue on. Secure. Glue on. Glue on. Glue flower on body. Sew on. 25.5 cm

Mane
Lightweight yarn Yellow 4 strands.
1→ ⟵ ⊗
⊢9.5= Chain 25. ⊣
|×| = Looped single crochet

Tail.
Dark Brown.
5 cm 0.7 cm 0.5 cm
Turn to right side.
4 cm Turn. 4 cm
Lightweight yarn Yellow 65 strands.
Fasten with cotton thread.
1 cm
Tuck in 1cm. Fasten with Yellow yarn.

(Child)

You'll Need Jersey 25cm square Red, 8cm square White. Felt: 6cm by 3cm Deep Pink. 5cm by 3cm Yellow Green. 4cm by 2cm Cherry Pink. Tangerine Yellow, Black, White small amount each. Lightweight yarn 10g. Yellow. 6-strand embroidery floss Red, Black small amount each. 30g. kapok. Glue. Crochet hook size 2/C.

Finished Size Refer to chart.

Cutting
  Cut jersey with 0.5cm seam allowance, felt with no allowance.

Assembly Same as for mother.

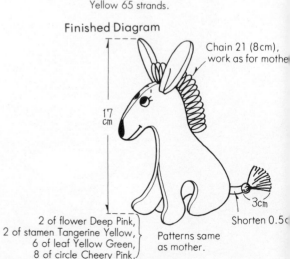

Finished Diagram
Chain 21 (8cm), work as for mother.
17 cm
3cm
Shorten 0.5c[m]
2 of flower Deep Pink,
2 of stamen Tangerine Yellow,
6 of leaf Yellow Green,
8 of circle Cheery Pink.
Patterns same as mother.

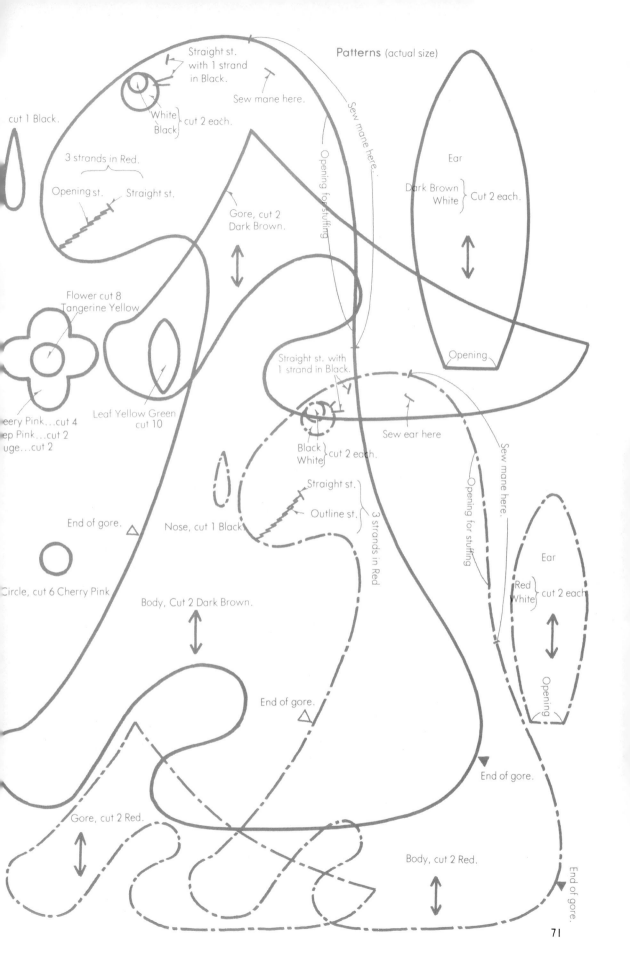

Patterns (actual size)

Straight st. with 1 strand in Black.

Sew mane here.

cut 1 Black.

White
Black } cut 2 each.

3 strands in Red.

Opening st.   Straight st.

Flower cut 8
Tangerine Yellow

Gore, cut 2
Dark Brown.

Sew mane here.

Opening for stuffing

Ear

Dark Brown
White } Cut 2 each.

Opening.

eery Pink…cut 4
ep Pink…cut 2
uge…cut 2

Leaf Yellow Green
cut 10

Straight st. with
1 strand in Black.

Black
White } cut 2 each.

Sew ear here

Straight st.

Outline st.

Sew mane here.

Opening for stuffing

End of gore.   △

Nose, cut 1 Black.

3 strands in Red

Ear

Red
White } cut 2 each

Circle, cut 6 Cherry Pink

Body, Cut 2 Dark Brown.

Opening

End of gore.   △

End of gore.   ▼

Gore, cut 2 Red.

Body, cut 2 Red.

End of gore.   ▼

Elephant & Horse

Instructions on pages 74 and 90.

Instructions on page 103.

Rabbit & Tiger

Elephant ⟷ shown on page 72

You'll Need Felt: 48cm by 44cm Gray. 11.5cm by 10cm Peacock Blue. 11cm by 5cm Cherry Pink. 16cm by 2.5cm White. 6cm by 4cm Dark Brown. 5cm by 3cm Black. Yellow Green small amount each. 6-strand embroidery floss Orange small amount. 0.6cm diameter spangle 16 of Plum, 2 of Black. 16 beads (large) White. Braid (see photo) 1.5cm wide by 24cm. Wire #24, 6cm. Small amount of floral tape Olive Green. 220g. kapok. **Finished Size** Refer to chart. **Cutting** Cut each piece with no seam allowance.

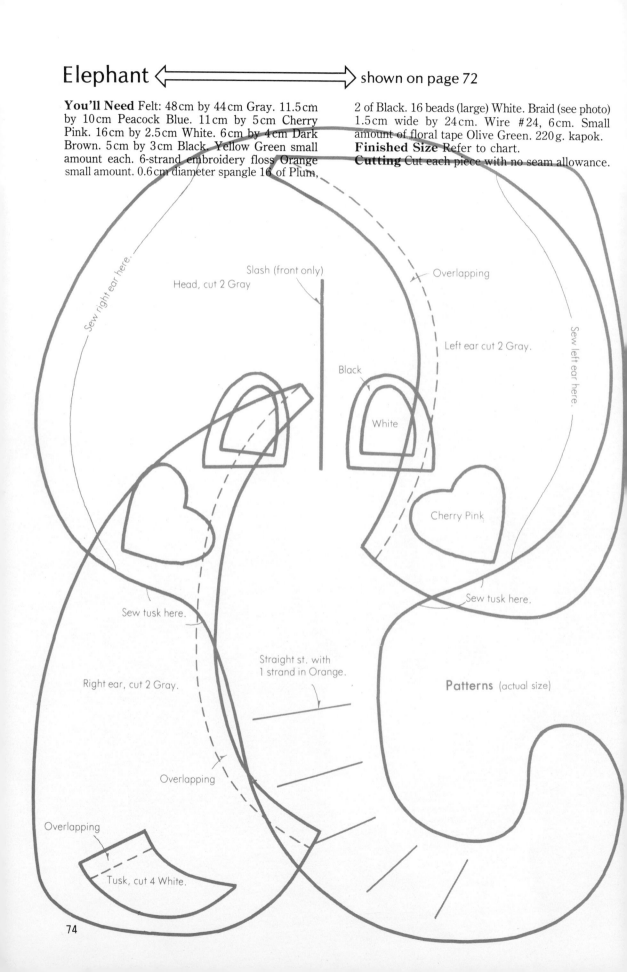

Sew right ear here.

Head, cut 2 Gray

Slash (front only)

Overlapping

Left ear cut 2 Gray.

Sew left ear here.

Black

White

Cherry Pink

Sew tusk here.

Sew tusk here.

Straight st. with 1 strand in Orange.

Right ear, cut 2 Gray.

Patterns (actual size)

Overlapping

Overlapping

Tusk, cut 4 White.

74

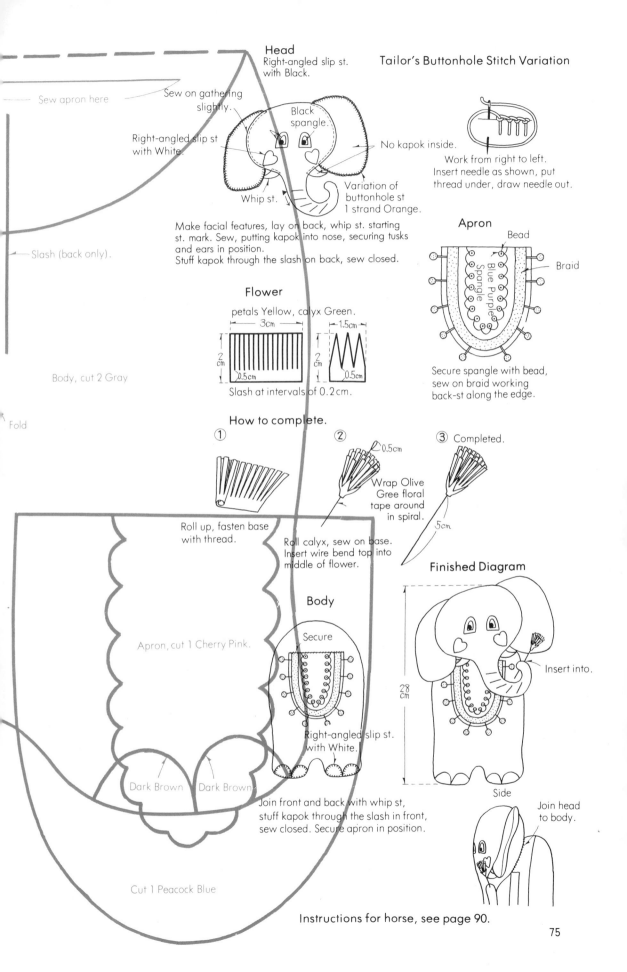

Head
Right-angled slip st.
with Black.

Tailor's Buttonhole Stitch Variation

Sew apron here

Sew on gathering
slightly.

Black
spangle.

Right-angled slip st
with White.

No kapok inside.

Work from right to left.
Insert needle as shown, put
thread under, draw needle out.

Whip st.

Variation of
buttonhole st
1 strand Orange.

Apron

Bead

Slash (back only).

Make facial features, lay on back, whip st. starting
st. mark. Sew, putting kapok into nose, securing tusks
and ears in position.
Stuff kapok through the slash on back, sew closed.

Blue Purple
Spangle

Braid

Flower

petals Yellow, calyx Green.

3cm

1.5cm

2 cm

2 cm

0.5cm

0.5cm

Body, cut 2 Gray

Secure spangle with bead,
sew on braid working
back-st along the edge.

Slash at intervals of 0.2cm.

Fold

How to complete.

① ② 0.5cm ③ Completed.

Roll up, fasten base
with thread.

Roll calyx, sew on base.
Insert wire bend top into
middle of flower.

Wrap Olive
Gree floral
tape around
in spiral.

5cm.

Finished Diagram

Body

Secure

Apron, cut 1 Cherry Pink.

Insert into.

28 cm

Right-angled slip st.
with White.

Dark Brown Dark Brown

Join front and back with whip st,
stuff kapok through the slash in front,
sew closed. Secure apron in position.

Side

Join head
to body.

Cut 1 Peacock Blue

Instructions for horse, see page 90.

75

BABY'S FAVORITE TOYS

Instructions on page 78.

Soft terry cloth feels good to a baby, and
tetoron batting, which is light and washable,
is good to use for baby's toys. But sew the
small parts firmly to the body, for a baby
loves to put things in his or her mouth.

Instructions on pages 79 and 91.

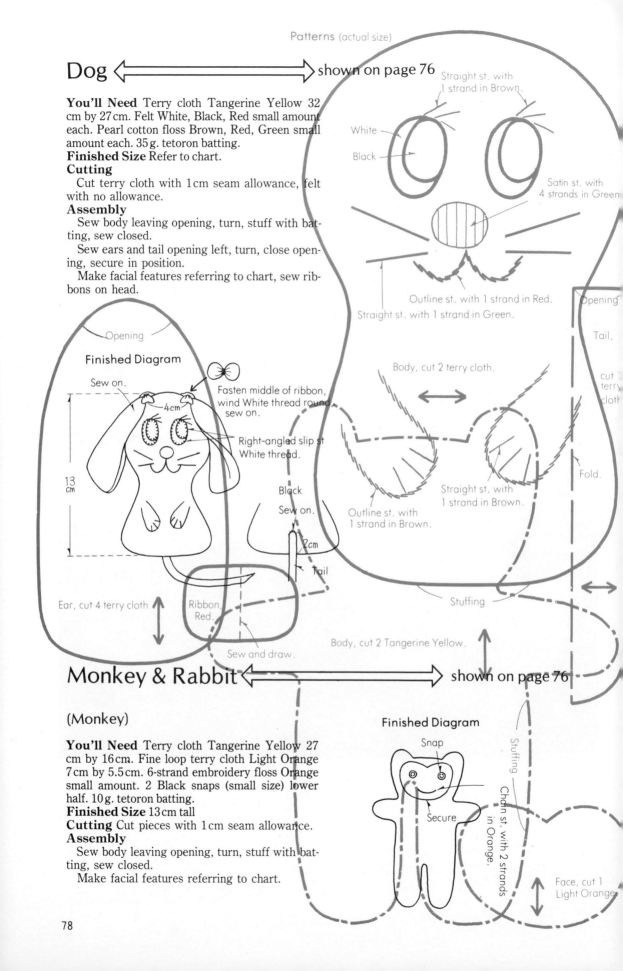

Dog ⟷ shown on page 76

You'll Need Terry cloth Tangerine Yellow 32 cm by 27 cm. Felt White, Black, Red small amount each. Pearl cotton floss Brown, Red, Green small amount each. 35 g. tetoron batting.
Finished Size Refer to chart.
Cutting
   Cut terry cloth with 1 cm seam allowance, felt with no allowance.
Assembly
   Sew body leaving opening, turn, stuff with batting, sew closed.
   Sew ears and tail opening left, turn, close opening, secure in position.
   Make facial features referring to chart, sew ribbons on head.

Straight st. with 1 strand in Brown.

White

Black

Satin st. with 4 strands in Green

Outline st. with 1 strand in Red.
Straight st. with 1 strand in Green.

Opening

Tail,

cut terry cloth

Body, cut 2 terry cloth.

Fold.

Straight st. with 1 strand in Brown.

Outline st. with 1 strand in Brown.

Stuffing

Body, cut 2 Tangerine Yellow.

Finished Diagram

Sew on.
4cm
Fasten middle of ribbon, wind White thread round, sew on.
Right-angled slip st White thread.
13 cm
Black
Sew on.
2cm
Tail
Ear, cut 4 terry cloth
Ribbon, Red.
Sew and draw.

Monkey & Rabbit ⟷ shown on page 76

(Monkey)

You'll Need Terry cloth Tangerine Yellow 27 cm by 16 cm. Fine loop terry cloth Light Orange 7 cm by 5.5 cm. 6-strand embroidery floss Orange small amount. 2 Black snaps (small size) lower half. 10 g. tetoron batting.
Finished Size 13 cm tall
Cutting Cut pieces with 1 cm seam allowance.
Assembly
   Sew body leaving opening, turn, stuff with batting, sew closed.
   Make facial features referring to chart.

Finished Diagram

Snap
Secure
Stuffing
Chain st. with 2 strands in Orange.
Face, cut 1 Light Orange

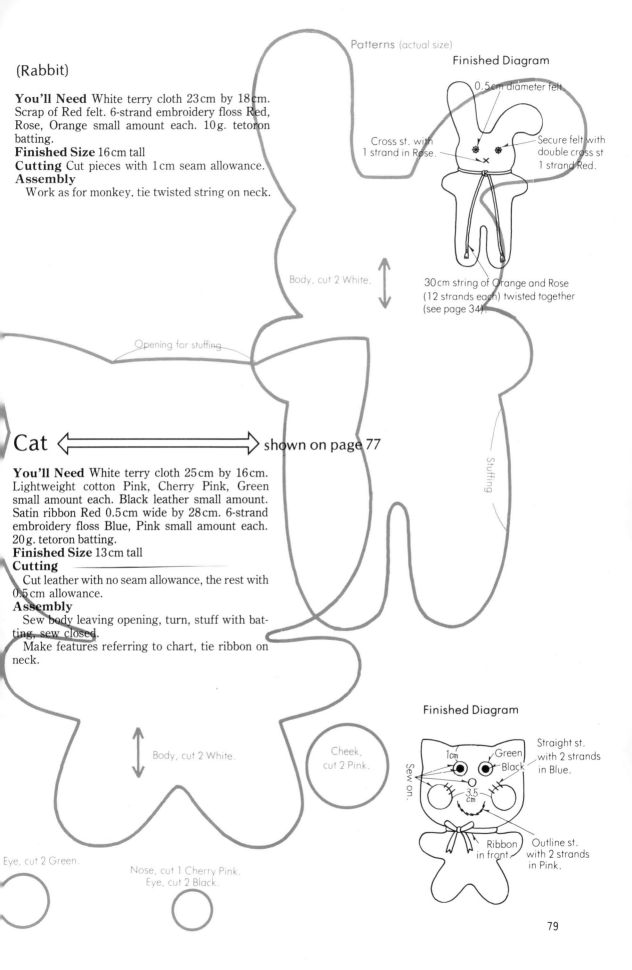

(Rabbit)

You'll Need White terry cloth 23 cm by 18 cm. Scrap of Red felt. 6-strand embroidery floss Red, Rose, Orange small amount each. 10 g. tetoron batting.

Finished Size 16 cm tall

Cutting Cut pieces with 1 cm seam allowance.

Assembly

Work as for monkey, tie twisted string on neck.

Patterns (actual size)

Finished Diagram

0.5 cm diameter felt.

Cross st. with 1 strand in Rose.

Secure felt with double cross st 1 strand Red.

Body, cut 2 White.

Opening for stuffing

30 cm string of Orange and Rose (12 strands each) twisted together (see page 34).

Stuffing

Cat ⟸⟹ shown on page 77

You'll Need White terry cloth 25 cm by 16 cm. Lightweight cotton Pink, Cherry Pink, Green small amount each. Black leather small amount. Satin ribbon Red 0.5 cm wide by 28 cm. 6-strand embroidery floss Blue, Pink small amount each. 20 g. tetoron batting.

Finished Size 13 cm tall

Cutting

Cut leather with no seam allowance, the rest with 0.5 cm allowance.

Assembly

Sew body leaving opening, turn, stuff with batting, sew closed.

Make features referring to chart, tie ribbon on neck.

Finished Diagram

Body, cut 2 White.

Cheek, cut 2 Pink.

Sew on.

1 cm

Green
Black

Straight st. with 2 strands in Blue.

3.5 cm

Ribbon in front.

Outline st. with 2 strands in Pink.

Eye, cut 2 Green.

Nose, cut 1 Cherry Pink.
Eye, cut 2 Black.

Instructions on page 81.

Monkey & Bear 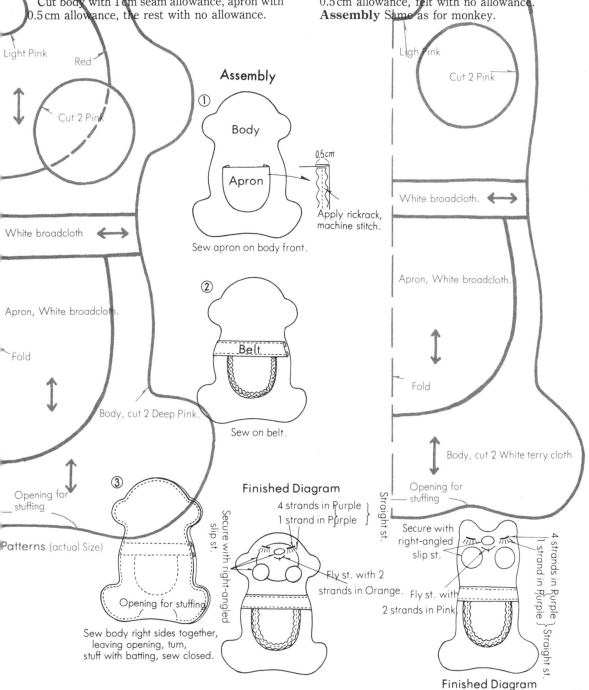 shown on page 80

(Monkey)

You'll Need 1 piece of toweling Deep Pink. Terry cloth Red 6.5 cm by 6 cm. White broadcloth 10 cm by 9 cm. Felt 6 cm by 3 cm Pink, Light Pink small amount. Red rickrack 0.3 cm wide by 15 cm. 6-strand embroidery floss Purple, Orange small amount each. 15 g. tetoron batting.
Finished Size 15.5 cm tall
Cutting
   Cut body with 1 cm seam allowance, apron with 0.5 cm allowance, the rest with no allowance.

(Bear)

You'll Need 1 piece of toweling White. White broadcloth 10 cm by 9 cm. Felt 6 cm by 3 cm Pink, Light Pink small amount, Red rickrack 0.3 cm wide by 15 cm. 6-strand embroidery floss Purple, Pink small amount each. 15 g. tetoron batting.
Finished Size 15.5 cm tall
Cutting
   Cut body with 1 cm seam allownace, apron with 0.5 cm allowance, felt with no allowance.
Assembly Same as for monkey.

Light Pink

Red

Cut 2 Pink

White broadcloth

Apron, White broadcloth.

Fold

Opening for stuffing

Patterns (actual size)

Light Pink

Cut 2 Pink

White broadcloth.

Apron, White broadcloth.

Fold

Body, cut 2 White terry cloth

Opening for stuffing

Assembly

① Body / Apron
0.5 cm
Apply rickrack, machine stitch.
Sew apron on body front.

② Belt
Sew on belt.

Body, cut 2 Deep Pink.

③ Opening for stuffing
Sew body right sides together, leaving opening, turn, stuff with batting, sew closed.

Finished Diagram

4 strands in Purple
1 strand in Purple
Secure with right-angled slip st.
Fly st. with 2 strands in Orange.

Straight st.

Secure with right-angled slip st.
4 strands in Purple
1 strand in Purple
Straight st.
Fly st. with 2 strands in Pink.

Finished Diagram

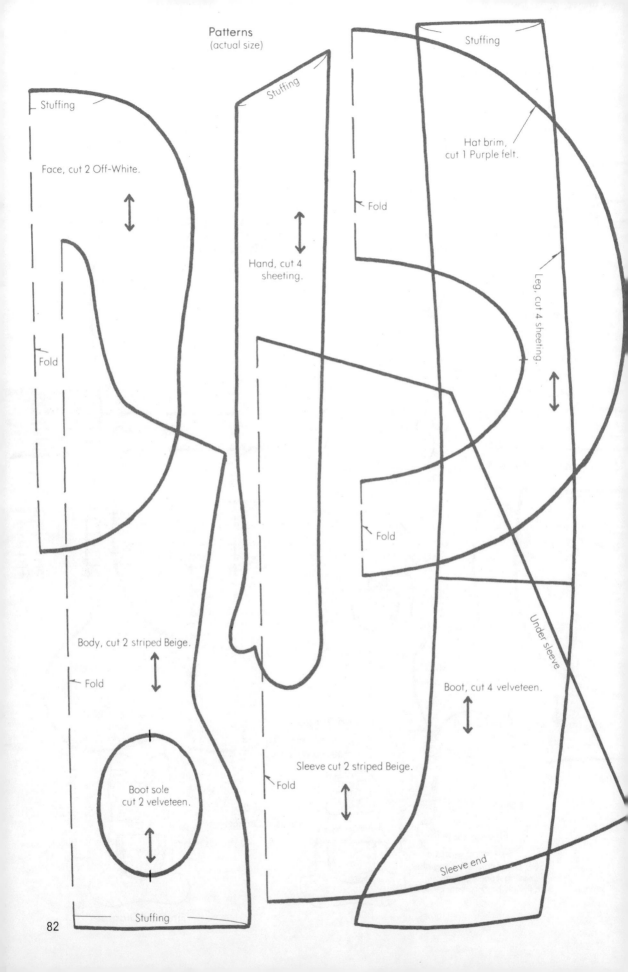

Patterns
(actual size)

Stuffing

Face, cut 2 Off-White.

Fold

Fold

Body, cut 2 striped Beige.

Fold

Boot sole
cut 2 velveteen.

Stuffing

82

Stuffing

Hand, cut 4
sheeting.

Fold

Fold

Sleeve cut 2 striped Beige.

Fold

Sleeve end

Stuffing

Hat brim,
cut 1 Purple felt.

Leg, cut 4 sheeting.

Under sleeve

Boot, cut 4 velveteen.

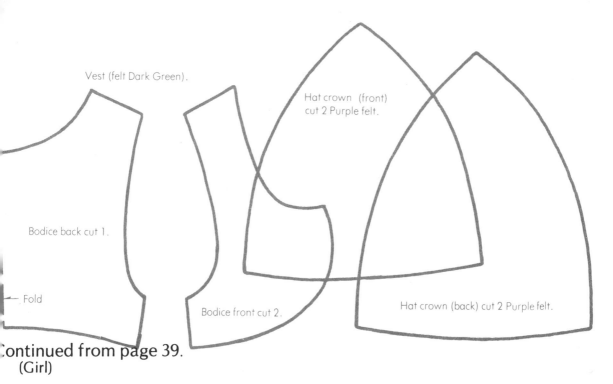

Vest (felt Dark Green).

Hat crown (front) cut 2 Purple felt.

Bodice back cut 1.

← Fold

Bodice front cut 2.

Hat crown (back) cut 2 Purple felt.

Continued from page 39.
(Girl)

You'll Need Lightweight wool White 25 cm by 22 cm. Velveteen 28 cm wide by 17 cm Orange, 13 cm by 10 cm Black. Red cotton print 53 cm by 15 cm. Felt Black, Deep Pink small amount each. Trimming lace Orange 0.8 cm wide by 124 cm.

Head, hands, and eyes

same color as boy,
heart on breast Deep Pink,
sleeves cotton print.
} Patterns same as boy.

2 of body (back pattern of boy) velveteen Orange.
Shoes same color as for boy.

① ~ ⑤ Work as for boy.

Mohair 15 g. Yellow. 6-strand embroidery floss Red, Brown small amount each. 100 g. kapok. Glue.
Finished Size 27 cm tall
Cutting
 Cut felt with no seam allowance, the rest with 1 cm allowance.

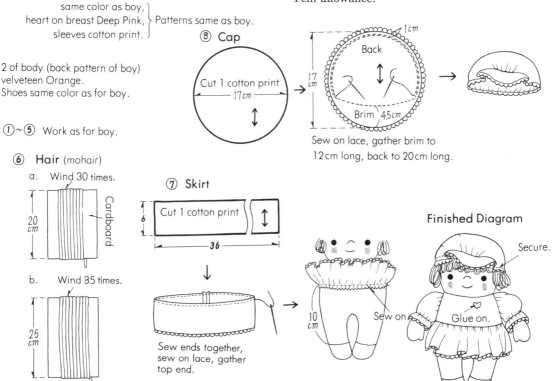

⑧ **Cap**

Cut 1 cotton print — 17 cm

Back

Brim 4.5 cm

17 cm

1 cm

Sew on lace, gather brim to 12 cm long, back to 20 cm long.

⑥ **Hair** (mohair)
 a. Wind 30 times.

20 cm — Cardboard

 b. Wind 35 times.

25 cm

Sew on 2 pieces (a and b) as for boy.

⑦ **Skirt**

Cut 1 cotton print
6
— 36 —

Sew ends together, sew on lace, gather top end.

10 cm

Sew on

Finished Diagram

Secure.

Glue on.

Doll (pair) ⟨⟶⟩ shown on page 37

(Boy)

You'll Need Sheeting 33 cm by 12.5 cm. Cotton fabric: 18 cm by 12.5 cm stripe of Red and White. 13 cm by 12.5 cm White print on Navy Blue. 9 cm by 7 cm Blue. Red, check of Red and White small amount each. Heavy duty yarn 50 g. Tangerine Yellow, 10 g. Orange. 6-strand embroidery floss Green small amount. 2 spangles star-shape 1 cm diameter Blue. 80 g. kapok.

Finished Size 29 cm tall

Cutting Cut each piece with no seam allowance.

Assembly

Sew with zigzag machine or open-buttonhole st.

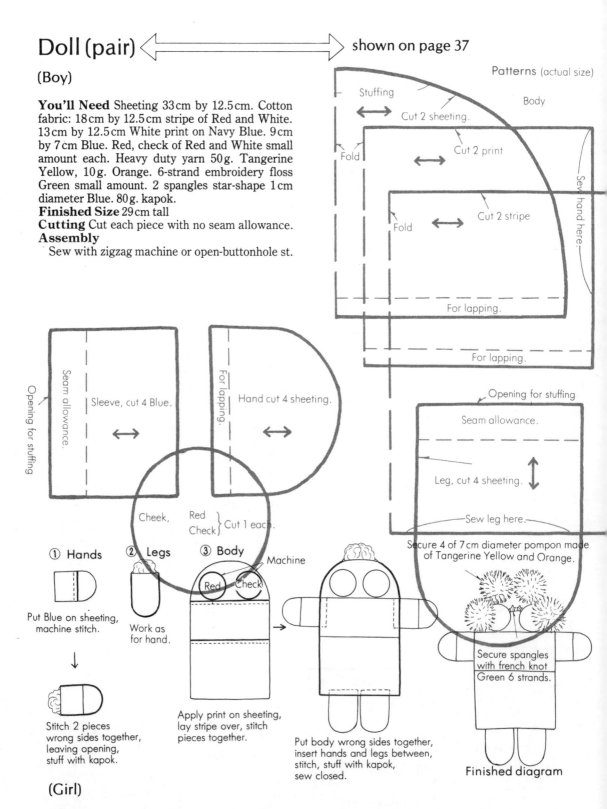

Patterns (actual size)

Stuffing

Body

Cut 2 sheeting.

Fold

Cut 2 print

Sew hand here.

Fold

Cut 2 stripe

For lapping.

For lapping.

Sleeve, cut 4 Blue.

Seam allowance.

Opening for stuffing

For lapping.

Hand cut 4 sheeting.

Opening for stuffing

Seam allowance.

Leg, cut 4 sheeting.

Sew leg here.

Cheek, Red Check } Cut 1 each.

Secure 4 of 7 cm diameter pompon made of Tangerine Yellow and Orange.

① Hands

② Legs

③ Body

Machine

Red Check

Put Blue on sheeting, machine stitch.

Work as for hand.

Secure spangles with french knot Green 6 strands.

Stitch 2 pieces wrong sides together, leaving opening, stuff with kapok.

Apply print on sheeting, lay stripe over, stitch pieces together.

Put body wrong sides together, insert hands and legs between, stitch, stuff with kapok, sew closed.

Finished diagram

(Girl)

You'll Need Sheeting 35 cm by 12.5 cm. Cotton fabric: 17 cm by 12.5 cm check of Red and White. 46 cm by 9.5 cm floral print. 7.5 cm by 12.5 cm stripe of Red and White. Heavy duty yarn 40 g. Red, 20 g. Wine Red. 6-strand embroidery floss Green small amount. 2 spangles star-shape 1 cm diameter Blue. 80 g. kapok.

Finished Size 30 cm tall

Cutting Cut each piece with no seam allowance.

Assembly Work as for boy.

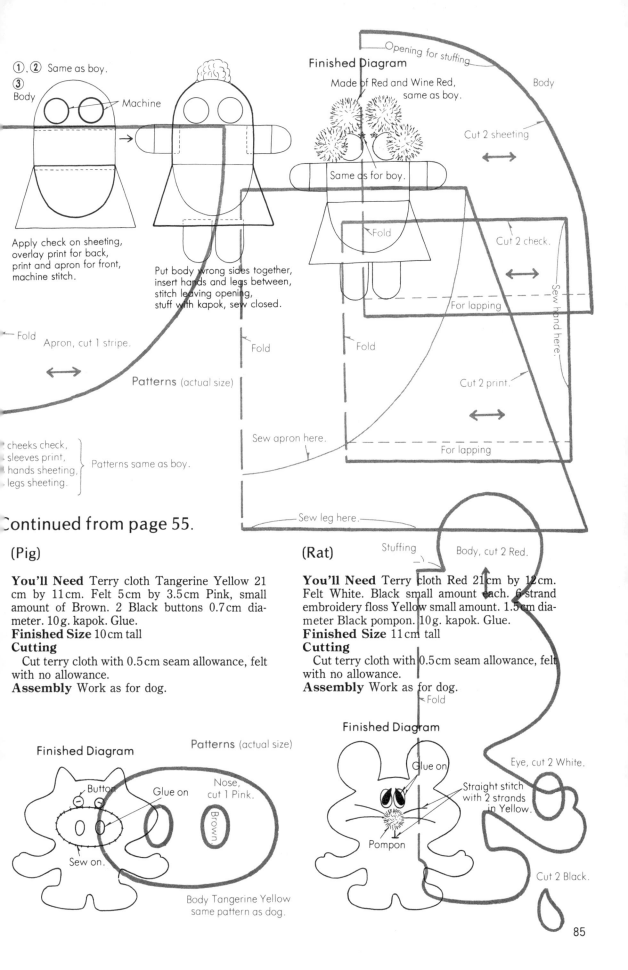

①.② Same as boy.

③ Body

Machine

Apply check on sheeting, overlay print for back, print and apron for front, machine stitch.

Put body wrong sides together, insert hands and legs between, stitch leaving opening, stuff with kapok, sew closed.

Fold

Apron, cut 1 stripe.

Patterns (actual size)

cheeks check, sleeves print, hands sheeting, legs sheeting.
} Patterns same as boy.

Finished Diagram
Made of Red and Wine Red, same as boy.

Opening for stuffing

Body

Cut 2 sheeting

Same as for boy.

Fold

Cut 2 check.

For lapping

Sew hand here.

Fold

Fold

Cut 2 print.

Sew apron here.

For lapping

Sew leg here.

Stuffing

Body, cut 2 Red.

Continued from page 55.

(Pig)

You'll Need Terry cloth Tangerine Yellow 21 cm by 11 cm. Felt 5 cm by 3.5 cm Pink, small amount of Brown. 2 Black buttons 0.7 cm diameter. 10 g. kapok. Glue.
Finished Size 10 cm tall
Cutting
   Cut terry cloth with 0.5 cm seam allowance, felt with no allowance.
Assembly Work as for dog.

(Rat)

You'll Need Terry cloth Red 21 cm by 12 cm. Felt White. Black small amount each. 6 strand embroidery floss Yellow small amount. 1.5 cm diameter Black pompon. 10 g. kapok. Glue.
Finished Size 11 cm tall
Cutting
   Cut terry cloth with 0.5 cm seam allowance, felt with no allowance.
Assembly Work as for dog.

Fold

Finished Diagram

Patterns (actual size)

Button

Glue on

Nose, cut 1 Pink.

Brown.

Sew on.

Body Tangerine Yellow same pattern as dog.

Finished Diagram

Glue on

Eye, cut 2 White.

Straight stitch with 2 strands in Yellow.

Pompon

Cut 2 Black.

Hippo & Cow

shown on page 41

Patterns (actual size)

Finished Diagram

(Hippo)

You'll Need Terry cloth Blue 40 cm by 25 cm. Felt Yellow, Black, Tomato Red small amount each. 6-strand embroidery floss Pink small amount. 35 g. kapok.

Finished Size Refer to chart.

Cutting

Cut terry cloth with 1 cm seam allowance, felt with no allowance.

Assembly

Sew body, hands opening left, turn, stuff with kapok, sew closed. Sew ears, turn, sew opening closed.

Secure ears and hands in position, make facial features referring to chart.

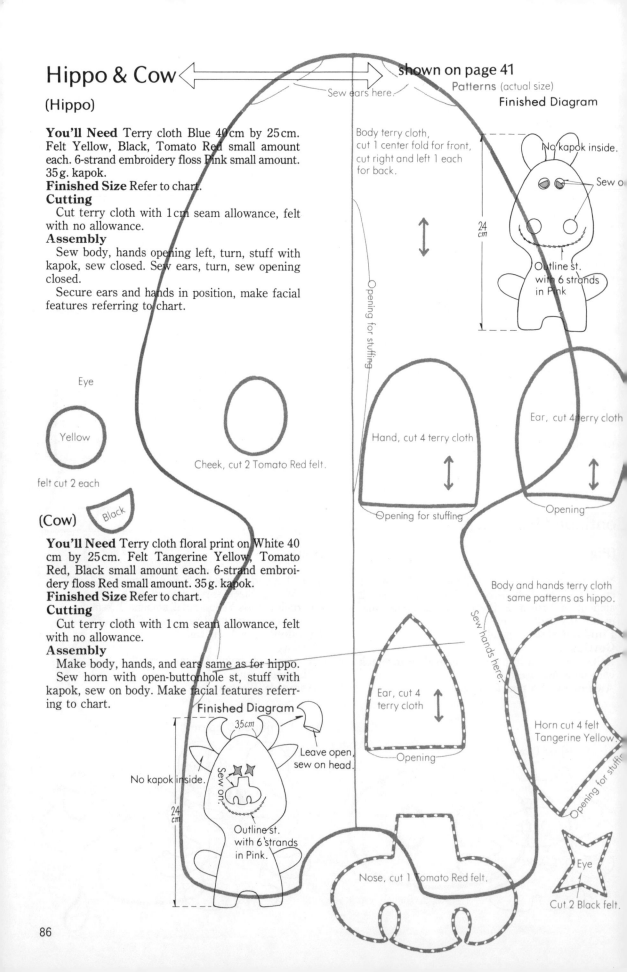

Sew ears here.

Body terry cloth, cut 1 center fold for front, cut right and left 1 each for back.

No kapok inside.

Sew o

24 cm

Outline st. with 6 strands in Pink

Opening for stuffing

Eye

Yellow

felt cut 2 each

Black

Cheek, cut 2 Tomato Red felt.

Hand, cut 4 terry cloth

Ear, cut 4 terry cloth

Opening for stuffing

Opening

(Cow)

You'll Need Terry cloth floral print on White 40 cm by 25 cm. Felt Tangerine Yellow, Tomato Red, Black small amount each. 6-strand embroidery floss Red small amount. 35 g. kapok.

Finished Size Refer to chart.

Cutting

Cut terry cloth with 1 cm seam allowance, felt with no allowance.

Assembly

Make body, hands, and ears same as for hippo.

Sew horn with open-buttonhole st, stuff with kapok, sew on body. Make facial features referring to chart.

Body and hands terry cloth same patterns as hippo.

Sew hands here.

Finished Diagram

3.5 cm

Leave open, sew on head.

No kapok inside.

Sew on.

24 cm

Outline st. with 6 strands in Pink.

Ear, cut 4 terry cloth

Opening

Horn cut 4 felt Tangerine Yellow

Opening for stuffing

Nose, cut 1 Tomato Red felt.

Eye

Cut 2 Black felt.

Rabbit & Monkey

Patterns (actual size) shown on page 65

Head, cut 2 Deep Pink.

(Rabbit)

You'll Need Broadcloth Deep Pink 64 cm by 18 cm. Cotton print 38 cm by 22 cm Pink, 20 cm by 10 cm Red, Yellow small amount. 40 pieces (various in prints) of 7 cm square cotton print for body. Scraps of White felt. 6-strand embroidery floss Black small amount. Purple rickrack 0.5 cm wide by 62 cm. 2 Red buttons 1.8 cm diameter. Cardboard. 250 g. tetoron batting.
Finished Size Refer to chart.
Cutting
Cut head, nose, cheeks, and ears with 1 cm seam allowance, eyes with no allowance.

Body:
2 pieces (patchwork of prints). Cut out 7 cm square pieces, patch with 0.5 cm allowance.

6 cm

3 cm

Fold

① Head

Seam.

Body

Stuffing

Sew right sides together, turn, stuff with batting, sew closed.

② Ear

Stuff lightly with kapok, stitch, tuck in allowance, draw.

Nose cut 1 each of Yellow print, cardboard.

Cheek, cut 2 Red print.

Finished Diagram

Apply batting sparsely on cardboard, lay fabric over, sew on.

Button

Sew on.

Straight st. embroidery floss 3 strands.

Rickrack

Outline st embroidery floss 3 strands.

39 cm

Eye, cut 2 White felt.

Ear, cut 4 Pink print.

(Monkey)

You'll Need Broadcloth 83 cm by 18 cm **Moss Green**, 22 cm by 13 cm Red. Cotton print 20 cm by 10 cm Pink, Yellow small amount. 40 pieces (various in prints) of 7 cm square cotton print for body. White felt small amount. 6-strand embroidery floss Black small amount. Yellow rickrack 0.5 cm wide by 62 cm. 2 Black buttons 1.8 cm diameter. Cardboard. 250 g. tetoron batting.
Finished Size Refer to chart.
Cutting
Cut head, face, nose, cheeks, and ears with 1 cm seam allowance, eyes with no allowance.

① Make body and head referring to (1) of rabbit.

② Ears:

Body prints (see photo), head Moss Green, cheeks Pink print, nose Yellow print, Eyes White felt.

} Patterns same as rabbit.

Stuffing

Stuff batting in lightly, sew closed.

Finished Diagram

Apply batting sparsely on cardboard, lay fabric over, sew on.

Button

Sew on.

③ Sew on.

Face

Ear

Rickrack

Outline st embroidery floss 3 strands.

39 cm

Face, cut 1 Red.

Ear, cut 4 Moss Green.

Fold

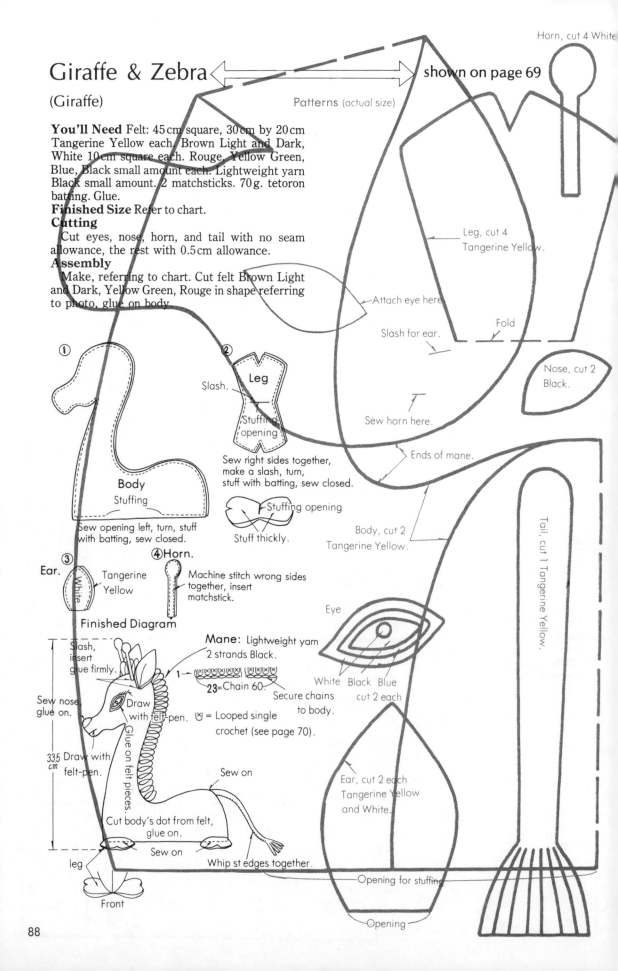

Giraffe & Zebra

shown on page 69

(Giraffe)

Patterns (actual size)

You'll Need Felt: 45 cm square, 30 cm by 20 cm Tangerine Yellow each, Brown Light and Dark, White 10 cm square each. Rouge, Yellow Green, Blue, Black small amount each. Lightweight yarn Black small amount. 2 matchsticks. 70 g. tetoron batting. Glue.

Finished Size Refer to chart.

Cutting
Cut eyes, nose, horn, and tail with no seam allowance, the rest with 0.5 cm allowance.

Assembly
Make, referring to chart. Cut felt Brown Light and Dark, Yellow Green, Rouge in shape referring to photo, glue on body.

Horn, cut 4 White

Leg, cut 4
Tangerine Yellow.

Attach eye here.

Slash for ear.

Fold

Nose, cut 2
Black.

Sew horn here.

Ends of mane.

Body, cut 2
Tangerine Yellow.

Tail, cut 1 Tangerine Yellow.

① Body
Stuffing
Sew opening left, turn, stuff with batting, sew closed.

② Leg
Slash.
Stuffing opening
Sew right sides together, make a slash, turn, stuff with batting, sew closed.

Stuffing opening
Stuff thickly.

③ Ear.
White
Tangerine Yellow

④ Horn.
Machine stitch wrong sides together, insert matchstick.

Eye
White Black Blue
cut 2 each

Finished Diagram

Slash, insert glue firmly.

Sew nose, glue on.

33.5 cm Draw with felt-pen.

Draw with felt-pen.

Glue on felt pieces.

Mane: Lightweight yarn 2 strands Black.
1 →
23 = Chain 60.
Secure chains to body.
☒ = Looped single crochet (see page 70).

Sew on

Cut body's dot from felt, glue on.

Sew on

Whip st edges together.

leg

Front

Ear, cut 2 each
Tangerine Yellow
and White.

Opening for stuffing

Opening

88

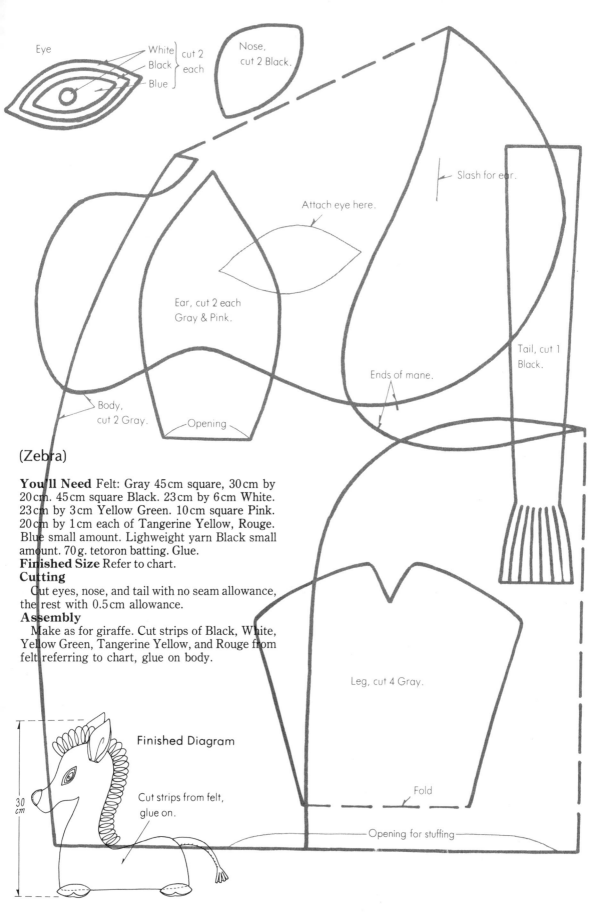

Eye

White
Black   cut 2
Blue   each

Nose, cut 2 Black.

Slash for ear.

Attach eye here.

Ear, cut 2 each
Gray & Pink.

Tail, cut 1
Black.

Ends of mane.

Body,
cut 2 Gray.

Opening

(Zebra)

You'll Need Felt: Gray 45 cm square, 30 cm by
20 cm. 45 cm square Black. 23 cm by 6 cm White.
23 cm by 3 cm Yellow Green. 10 cm square Pink.
20 cm by 1 cm each of Tangerine Yellow, Rouge.
Blue small amount. Lighweight yarn Black small
amount. 70 g. tetoron batting. Glue.
Finished Size Refer to chart.
Cutting
   Cut eyes, nose, and tail with no seam allowance,
the rest with 0.5 cm allowance.
Assembly
   Make as for giraffe. Cut strips of Black, White,
Yellow Green, Tangerine Yellow, and Rouge from
felt referring to chart, glue on body.

Leg, cut 4 Gray.

Finished Diagram

Cut strips from felt,
glue on.

30 cm

Fold

Opening for stuffing

Horse ⟵⟶ shown on page 72

You'll Need Cotton velour Red 60 cm by 35 cm.
White cotton lace 4.5 cm wide by 50 cm, 1.2 cm
wide by 84 cm. Tussore broad Yellow Green 12 cm
by 8 cm. Blue felt small amount. Sport weight
yarn Blue, Pink, Mauve, Reddish Purple, Greenish
Brown, Purple, Yellow Green small amount each.
6-strand embroidery floss Blue small amount. 120
g. kapok.
Finished Size Refer to chart.
Cutting
   Eyes with no seam allowance, the rest with 1 cm
allowance.

① Sew head gore here. Body. Sew along where indicated right sides together.

② Gore of head. Sew gore to head.

③ Gore of legs. Stuffing. Sew right sides together opening left.

④ Body. Gore of legs. Sew gore of legs on body.

Mane: Fold 50 cm lace in half, gather up to 13 cm long. Wrong side 4.5 cm. Turn to right side. (Sew flower A, B, and C on the other side.)

⑤ Ear. Yellow Green. Red. → Turn right side out.

Flower, sport weight yarn 1 strand.

Coloring:

	A	B	C	D	E	F
1st row	Yellow Green	"	"	"	"	"
2nd row	Blue	Pink	Mauve	Reddish Purple	Greenish Brown	Purple

Finished Diagram

Right side. Secure. Right-angled slip st embroidery floss 2 strands Blue! 20 cm. D E F B C A Secure. Sew on. Fold 6 strips of lace 1.2 cm wide by 14 cm in half.

Patterns (actual size)

Ends of Legs gore.

Ear, cut 2 each Red & Yellow Green.

Opening

Legs gore cut 2 Red.

Body, cut 2 Red.

Stuffing

Eye, cut 2 felt.

Ends of head gore.

Head gore, cut 1 Red.

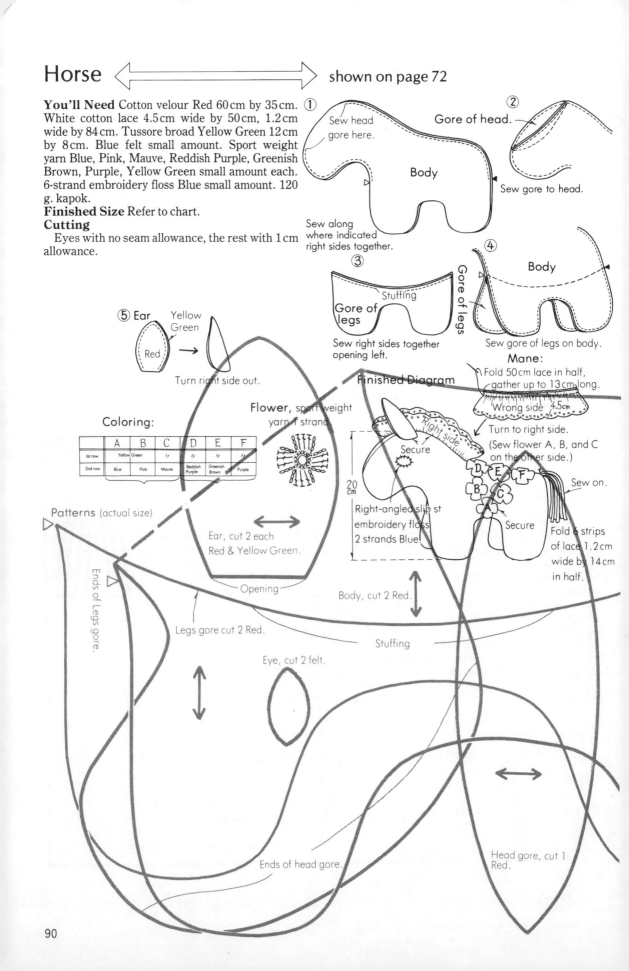

90

Duckling & Fish

shown on page 77

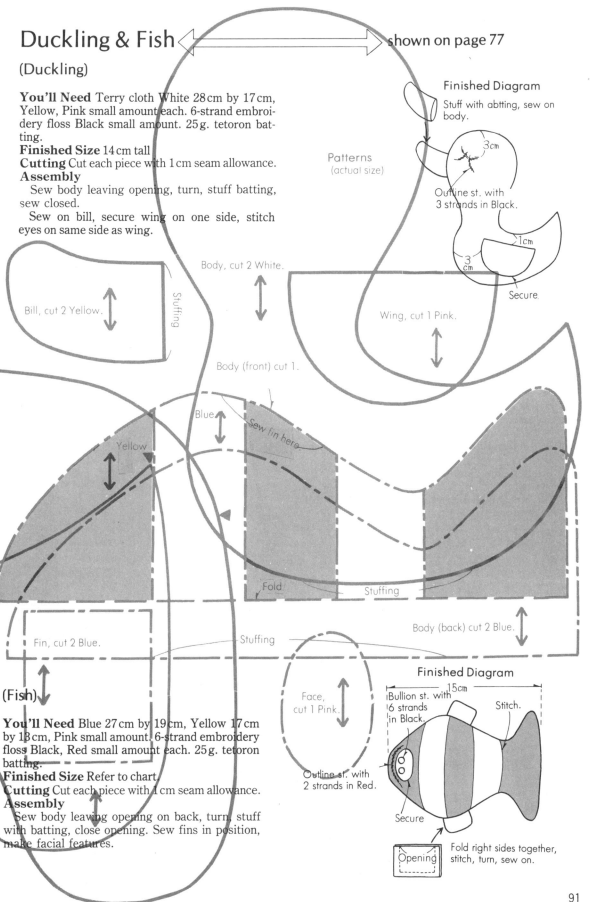

(Duckling)

You'll Need Terry cloth White 28 cm by 17 cm, Yellow, Pink small amount each. 6-strand embroidery floss Black small amount. 25 g. tetoron batting.

Finished Size 14 cm tall

Cutting Cut each piece with 1 cm seam allowance.

Assembly

Sew body leaving opening, turn, stuff batting, sew closed.

Sew on bill, secure wing on one side, stitch eyes on same side as wing.

Patterns
(actual size)

Finished Diagram
Stuff with abtting, sew on body.

3 cm

Outline st. with 3 strands in Black.

1 cm

3 cm

Secure

Bill, cut 2 Yellow.

Stuffing

Body, cut 2 White.

Wing, cut 1 Pink.

Body (front) cut 1.

Blue

Sew fin here

Yellow

Fold

Stuffing

Body (back) cut 2 Blue.

Fin, cut 2 Blue.

Stuffing

Face, cut 1 Pink.

(Fish)

You'll Need Blue 27 cm by 19 cm, Yellow 17 cm by 13 cm, Pink small amount. 6-strand embroidery floss Black, Red small amount each. 25 g. tetoron batting.

Finished Size Refer to chart.

Cutting Cut each piece with 1 cm seam allowance.

Assembly

Sew body leaving opening on back, turn, stuff with batting, close opening. Sew fins in position, make facial features.

Outline st. with 2 strands in Red.

Finished Diagram

15 cm

Bullion st. with 6 strands in Black.

Stitch.

Secure

Opening

Fold right sides together, stitch, turn, sew on.

91

Continued from page 15.

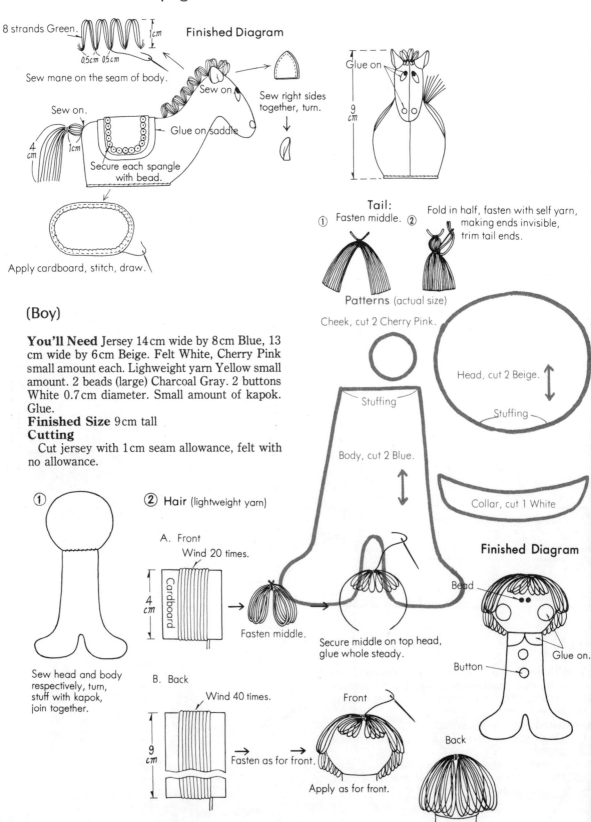

8 strands Green.

1cm

0.5cm 0.5cm

Sew mane on the seam of body.

Sew on.

Finished Diagram

Sew on.

Sew right sides together, turn.

4 cm   1cm

Glue on saddle

Secure each spangle with bead.

Apply cardboard, stitch, draw.

Glue on

9 cm

Tail:
① Fasten middle. ②

Fold in half, fasten with self yarn, making ends invisible, trim tail ends.

Patterns (actual size)

Cheek, cut 2 Cherry Pink.

(Boy)

You'll Need Jersey 14cm wide by 8cm Blue, 13 cm wide by 6cm Beige. Felt White, Cherry Pink small amount each. Lighweight yarn Yellow small amount. 2 beads (large) Charcoal Gray. 2 buttons White 0.7cm diameter. Small amount of kapok. Glue.

Finished Size 9cm tall

Cutting

Cut jersey with 1cm seam allowance, felt with no allowance.

Head, cut 2 Beige.

Stuffing

Stuffing

Body, cut 2 Blue.

Collar, cut 1 White.

Finished Diagram

① Sew head and body respectively, turn, stuff with kapok, join together.

② **Hair** (lightweight yarn)

A. Front

Wind 20 times.

Cardboard

4 cm

Fasten middle.

Secure middle on top head, glue whole steady.

Bead

Button

Glue on.

B. Back

Wind 40 times.

9 cm

Fasten as for front.

Apply as for front.

Front

Back

(Girl)

You'll Need Jersey Red 14cm wide by 8cm, Beige 13cm wide by 6cm. Felt Cherry Pink small amount. Lightweight yarn Yellow small amount. 2 beads (large) Charcoal Gray. Ribbon Orange 0.3cm wide by 14cm. White lace 1.5cm wide by 25cm. Small amount of kapok. Glue.

Finished Size 9cm tall

Cutting

Cut jersey with 1cm seam allowance, felt with no allowance.

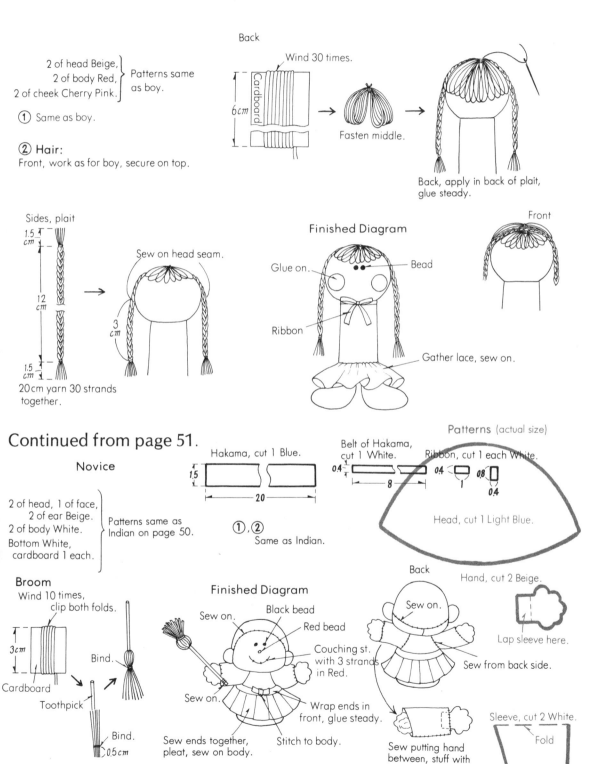

2 of head Beige,
2 of body Red,
2 of cheek Cherry Pink. } Patterns same as boy.

① Same as boy.

② Hair:
Front, work as for boy, secure on top.

Back

Wind 30 times.

Cardboard
6cm

Fasten middle.

Back, apply in back of plait, glue steady.

Sides, plait

1.5 cm
12 cm
1.5 cm

20cm yarn 30 strands together.

Sew on head seam.

3 cm

Finished Diagram

Front

Glue on.
Bead
Ribbon
Gather lace, sew on.

Continued from page 51.

Novice

2 of head, 1 of face,
2 of ear Beige.
2 of body White.
Bottom White,
cardboard 1 each. } Patterns same as Indian on page 50.

Hakama, cut 1 Blue.

1.5
20

Belt of Hakama, cut 1 White.
04
8

Ribbon, cut 1 each White.
04
1
08
04

Patterns (actual size)

Head, cut 1 Light Blue.

①,② Same as Indian.

Broom

Wind 10 times, clip both folds.

3cm
Cardboard
Toothpick
Bind.
Bind.
0.5cm

Finished Diagram

Sew on.
Black bead
Red bead
Couching st. with 3 strands in Red.
Wrap ends in front, glue steady.
Sew on.
Sew ends together, pleat, sew on body.
Stitch to body.

Back
Sew on.

Hand, cut 2 Beige.
Lap sleeve here.
Sew from back side.

Sew putting hand between, stuff with kapok.

Sleeve, cut 2 White.
Fold

Continued from page 19.

(Judy Abbott)

You'll Need Felt: 22 cm by 20 cm Cherry Pink. 20 cm by 15 cm Light Pink. 15 cm by 12 cm Light Moss Green. 10 cm by 4 cm White. White cotton lace 1.5 cm wide by 35 cm. White frill (see photo) 2.5 cm wide by 10 cm. Lightweight yarn Light Beige small amount. 6-strand embroidery floss Cherry Pink, Pink small amount each. Bead 2 of Black (mid size), 1 of Red (small size). 10 g. kapok. Glue.
Finished Size 25 cm tall
Cutting Cut each piece with no seam allowance.
Assembly
  Sew felt pieces with open-buttonhole stitch.

Patterns (actual size)

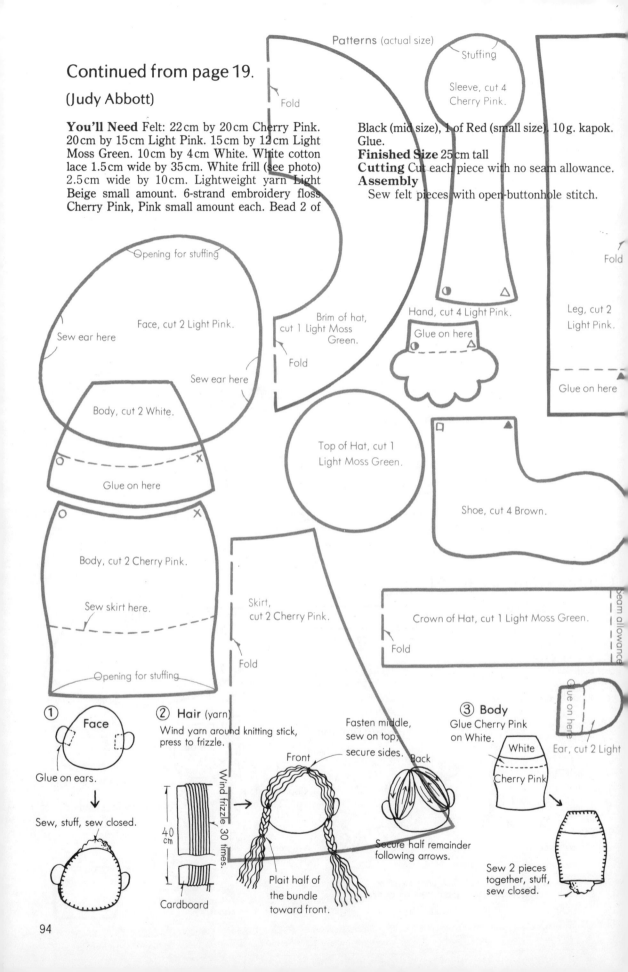

Fold

Stuffing
Sleeve, cut 4
Cherry Pink.

Fold

Opening for stuffing

Face, cut 2 Light Pink.

Sew ear here

Sew ear here

Brim of hat,
cut 1 Light Moss
Green.

Fold

Hand, cut 4 Light Pink.

Glue on here

Leg, cut 2
Light Pink.

Glue on here

Body, cut 2 White.

O   X

Glue on here

Top of Hat, cut 1
Light Moss Green.

Shoe, cut 4 Brown.

O   X

Body, cut 2 Cherry Pink.

Sew skirt here.

Skirt,
cut 2 Cherry Pink.

Crown of Hat, cut 1 Light Moss Green.

seam allowance

Fold

Opening for stuffing

Fold

Glue on here

① Face
Glue on ears.

↓

Sew, stuff, sew closed.

② Hair (yarn)
Wind yarn around knitting stick,
press to frizzle.

Wind frizzle 30 times.

40 cm

Cardboard

Front

Plait half of
the bundle
toward front.

Fasten middle,
sew on top,
secure sides.

Back

Secure half remainder
following arrows.

③ Body
Glue Cherry Pink
on White.

White

Cherry Pink

Ear, cut 2 Light

Sew 2 pieces
together, stuff,
sew closed.

④ Legs:

Stuff with kapok

Sew together.

Lap shoe here.

Glue shoe on, sew along.

Cross st 6 strands Pink.

⑤

Sew on.

Seam together

⑥

Secure

Skirt

⑦

Sleeve

Hand

Glue sleeve on hand.

Stuff with kapok, sew closed.

Sew 2 pieces together.

Sew on ⑧

Couching st. with 1 strand in Cherry Pink.

Black bead

Red bead

Tilt head to left, sew on body.

Glue on Pink felt frayed into fleece.

Front

Tie lace on waist.

Back

⑨

Sew on neck.

Ribbon in front.

Gather.

Frill

5

13

Cherry Pink

0.3

⑩ Hat:

Crown

Sew right sides together.

Turn to right side, join with top.

Sew to brim, apply on head.

Open buttonhole st. with 6 strands in Pink.

Girl's patterns on page 47.

Patterns (actual size)

Collar, cut 1 Orange.

Hat, cut 1 Orange.

For lapping.

Skirt, cut 2 Pink.

Fold

Fold

Shoe, cut 4 Orange.

Accent of shoes cut 2 Yellow.

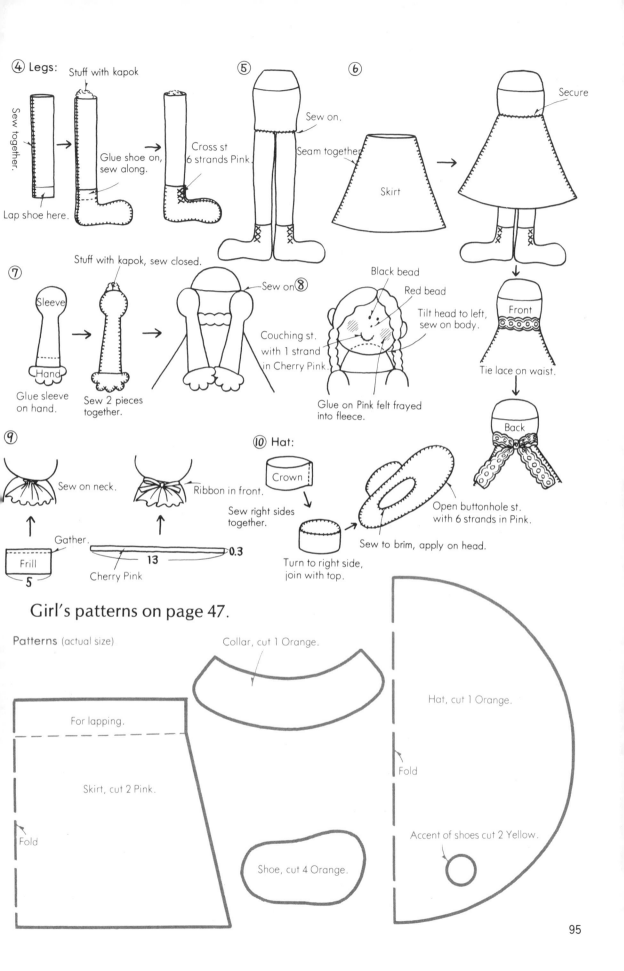

Continued from page 63.

(Below left)

You'll Need Striped jersey 16 cm wide by 7 cm. Felt: 10 cm square Orange. 5 cm by 4 cm Blue Green. Red, White small amount each. Heavy duty yarn Blue, Green 10 g. each. 6-strand embroidery floss Black small amount. 1.5 cm diameter pompon Dusty Green. Grosgrain ribbon Yellow 1.5 cm wide by 30 cm. 5 g. kapok. Glue.
Finished Size 16.5 cm tall
Cutting
  Cut jersey with 0.5 cm seam allowance, felt with no allowance.

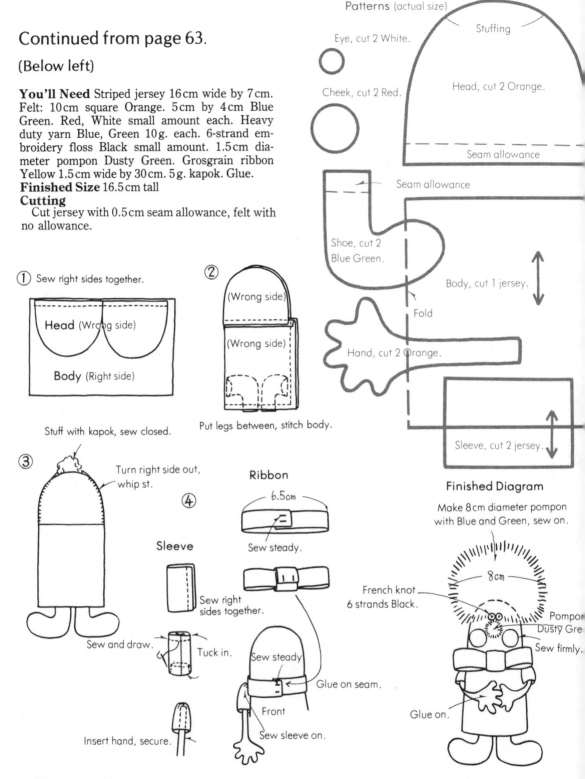

Patterns (actual size)

Eye, cut 2 White.

Cheek, cut 2 Red.

Stuffing

Head, cut 2 Orange.

Seam allowance

Seam allowance

Shoe, cut 2 Blue Green.

Body, cut 1 jersey.

Fold

Hand, cut 2 Orange.

Sleeve, cut 2 jersey.

① Sew right sides together.

Head (Wrong side)

Body (Right side)

Stuff with kapok, sew closed.

② (Wrong side) (Wrong side)

Put legs between, stitch body.

③ Stuff with kapok, sew closed.
Turn right side out, whip st.

④ Sew and draw. Tuck in.
Insert hand, secure.

Sleeve
Sew right sides together.

Ribbon
6.5 cm
Sew steady.

Sew steady
Front
Sew sleeve on.
Glue on seam.

Finished Diagram
Make 8 cm diameter pompon with Blue and Green, sew on.

8 cm

French knot 6 strands Black.

Pompon Dusty Green

Sew firmly.

Glue on.

(Below middle)

You'll Need Felt: 10 cm by 6 cm Red. 10 cm by 4.5 cm Light Beige. 5 cm by 4 cm Black. Orange, Gray Brown, White small amount each. 6-strand embroidery floss small amount Black. Gold tape 1 cm wide by 11 cm. Black cord 0.5 cm diameter by 12 cm. 5 of Silver button 1.2 cm diameter. 8 cm diameter fur pompon Black. 5 g. kapok. Glue.
Finished Size 17.5 cm tall
Cutting Cut each piece with no seam allowance.

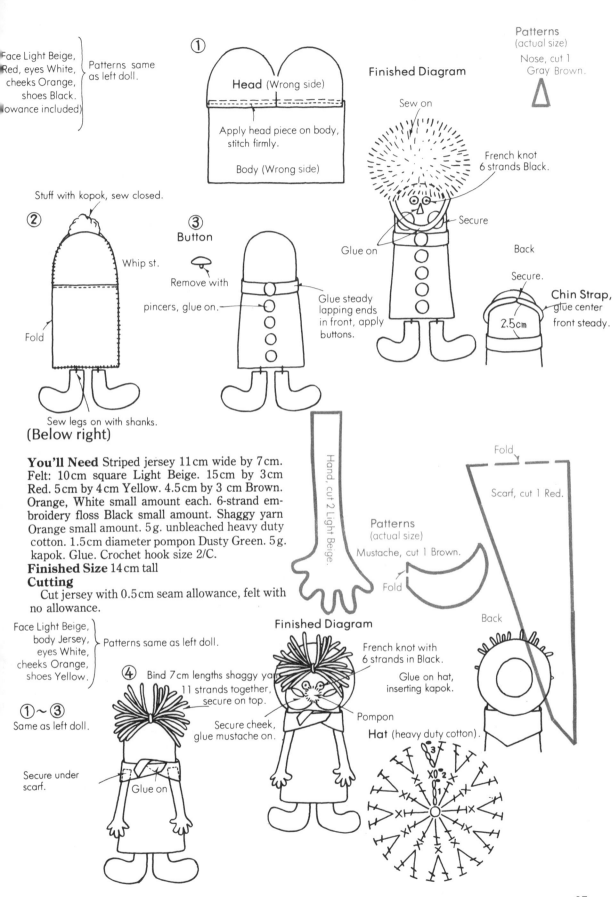

Face Light Beige, Red, eyes White, cheeks Orange, shoes Black. (allowance included)

Patterns same as left doll.

Patterns
(actual size)

Nose, cut 1
Gray Brown.

① Head (Wrong side)

Apply head piece on body, stitch firmly.

Body (Wrong side)

Finished Diagram

Sew on

French knot
6 strands Black.

Secure

Glue on

Back

Secure.

2.5cm

Chin Strap,
glue center
front steady.

Stuff with kopok, sew closed.

② Whip st.

Fold

Sew legs on with shanks.

③ **Button**

Remove with
pincers, glue on.

Glue steady
lapping ends
in front, apply
buttons.

(Below right)

You'll Need Striped jersey 11 cm wide by 7 cm. Felt: 10 cm square Light Beige. 15 cm by 3 cm Red. 5 cm by 4 cm Yellow. 4.5 cm by 3 cm Brown. Orange, White small amount each. 6-strand embroidery floss Black small amount. Shaggy yarn Orange small amount. 5 g. unbleached heavy duty cotton. 1.5 cm diameter pompon Dusty Green. 5 g. kapok. Glue. Crochet hook size 2/C.
Finished Size 14 cm tall
Cutting
Cut jersey with 0.5 cm seam allowance, felt with no allowance.

Hand, cut 2 Light Beige.

Fold

Scarf, cut 1 Red.

Patterns
(actual size)

Mustache, cut 1 Brown.

Fold

Back

Face Light Beige,
body Jersey,
eyes White,
cheeks Orange,
shoes Yellow.

Patterns same as left doll.

①~③
Same as left doll.

Secure under
scarf.

Finished Diagram

④ Bind 7cm lengths shaggy yarn
11 strands together,
secure on top.

Secure cheek,
glue mustache on.

Glue on

French knot with
6 strands in Black.

Glue on hat,
inserting kapok.

Pompon

Hat (heavy duty cotton).

3
X0 2
1

97

Mushlle ⟵⟶ shown on page 21

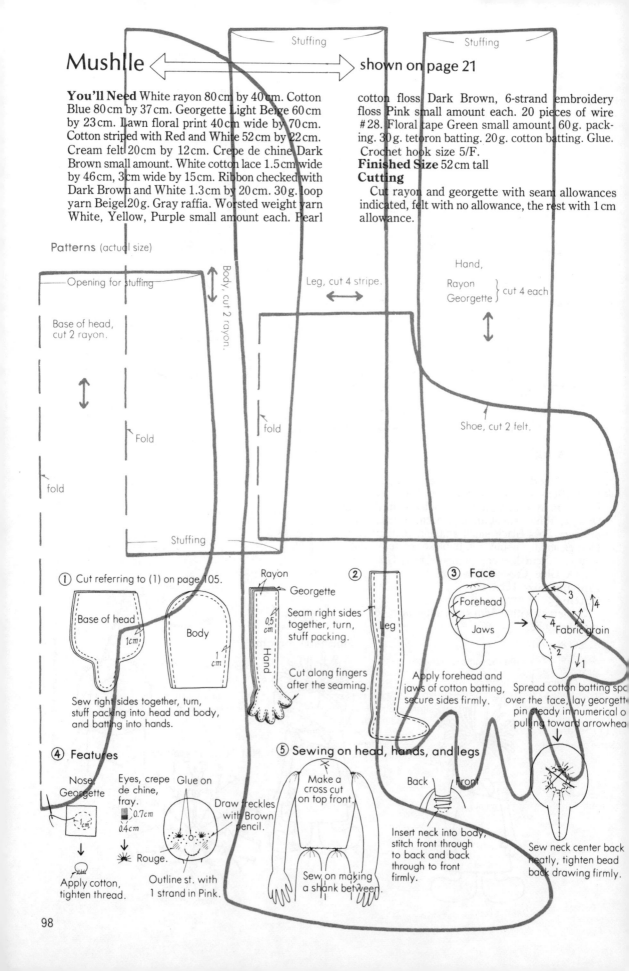

You'll Need White rayon 80 cm by 40 cm. Cotton Blue 80 cm by 37 cm. Georgette Light Beige 60 cm by 23 cm. Lawn floral print 40 cm wide by 70 cm. Cotton striped with Red and White 52 cm by 22 cm. Cream felt 20 cm by 12 cm. Crepe de chine Dark Brown small amount. White cotton lace 1.5 cm wide by 46 cm, 3 cm wide by 15 cm. Ribbon checked with Dark Brown and White 1.3 cm by 20 cm. 30 g. loop yarn Beige. 20 g. Gray raffia. Worsted weight yarn White, Yellow, Purple small amount each. Pearl cotton floss Dark Brown, 6-strand embroidery floss Pink small amount each. 20 pieces of wire #28. Floral tape Green small amount. 60 g. packing. 30 g. teteron batting. 20 g. cotton batting. Glue. Crochet hook size 5/F.

Finished Size 52 cm tall

Cutting

Cut rayon and georgette with seam allowances indicated, felt with no allowance, the rest with 1 cm allowance.

Patterns (actual size)

Opening for stuffing

Base of head, cut 2 rayon.

Body, cut 2 rayon.

Fold

fold

Stuffing

Stuffing

Leg, cut 4 stripe.

Hand, Rayon Georgette } cut 4 each

Shoe, cut 2 felt.

① Cut referring to (1) on page 105.

Base of head

1 cm

Body

1 cm

Sew right sides together, turn, stuff packing into head and body, and batting into hands.

Rayon

Georgette

0.5 cm

Hand

Seam right sides together, turn, stuff packing.

Cut along fingers after the seaming.

② Leg

③ Face

Forehead

Jaws

Apply forehead and jaws of cotton batting, secure sides firmly.

3 4 Fabric grain 4 2 1

Spread cotton batting spo over the face, lay georgette pin steady in numerical o pulling toward arrowhea

④ Features

Nose, Georgette

1 cm

Apply cotton, tighten thread.

Eyes, crepe de chine, fray. 0.7 cm 0.4 cm

Rouge.

Glue on

Draw freckles with Brown pencil.

Outline st. with 1 strand in Pink.

⑤ Sewing on head, hands, and legs

Make a cross cut on top front.

Sew on making a shank between.

Back Front

Insert neck into body, stitch front through to back and back through to front firmly.

Sew neck center back neatly, tighten bead back drawing firmly.

98

Cut out pieces of clothes

⑥ (Hem of skirt and bloomers with 1.5cm allowance, the rest with 1cm allowance.)

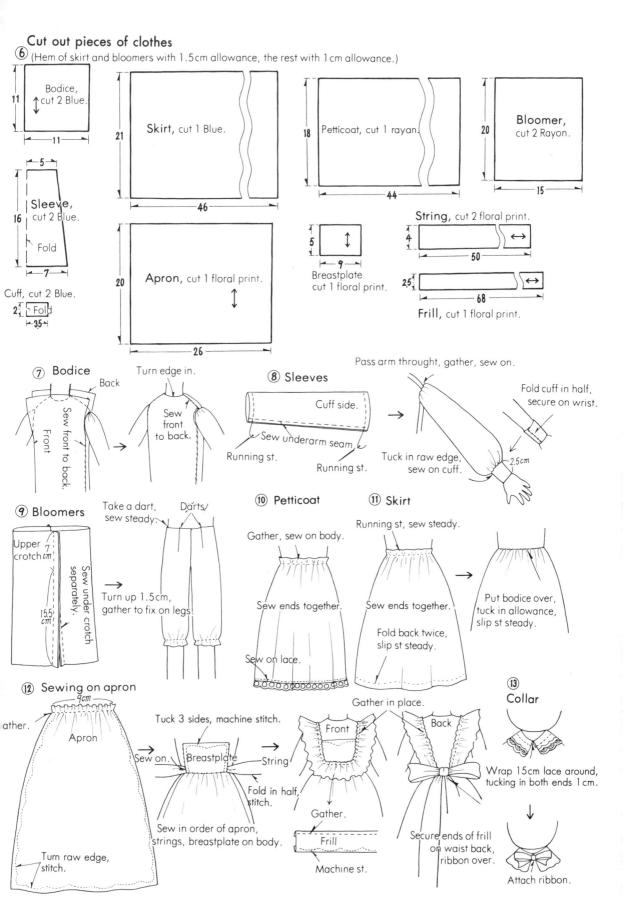

Bodice, cut 2 Blue. (11, 11)

Skirt, cut 1 Blue. (21, 46)

Petticoat, cut 1 rayan. (18, 44)

Bloomer, cut 2 Rayon. (20, 15)

Sleeve, cut 2 Blue. (5, 16, 7) Fold

Cuff, cut 2 Blue. (2, 35) Fold

Apron, cut 1 floral print. (20, 26)

Breastplate cut 1 floral print. (5, 9)

String, cut 2 floral print. (4, 50)

Frill, cut 1 floral print. (2.5, 68)

⑦ Bodice

Back — Turn edge in.
Sew front to back. Front
Sew front to back.

⑧ Sleeves

Pass arm throught, gather, sew on.
Cuff side.
Sew underarm seam. Running st. Running st.
Fold cuff in half, secure on wrist.
Tuck in raw edge, sew on cuff. 2.5cm

⑨ Bloomers

Upper crotch 7cm
Sew under crotch separately.
15.5cm
Take a dart, sew steady. Darts
Turn up 1.5cm, gather to fix on legs.

⑩ Petticoat

Gather, sew on body.
Sew ends together.
Sew on lace.

⑪ Skirt

Running st, sew steady.
Sew ends together.
Fold back twice, slip st steady.
Put bodice over, tuck in allowance, slip st steady.

⑫ Sewing on apron

9cm
Gather. Apron
Turn raw edge, stitch.
Sew on.
Tuck 3 sides, machine stitch.
Breastplate — String
Fold in half, stitch.
Sew in order of apron, strings, breastplate on body.
Gather in place. Front
Gather.
Frill
Machine st.
Back
Secure ends of frill on waist back, ribbon over.

⑬ Collar

Wrap 15cm lace around, tucking in both ends 1cm.
Attach ribbon.

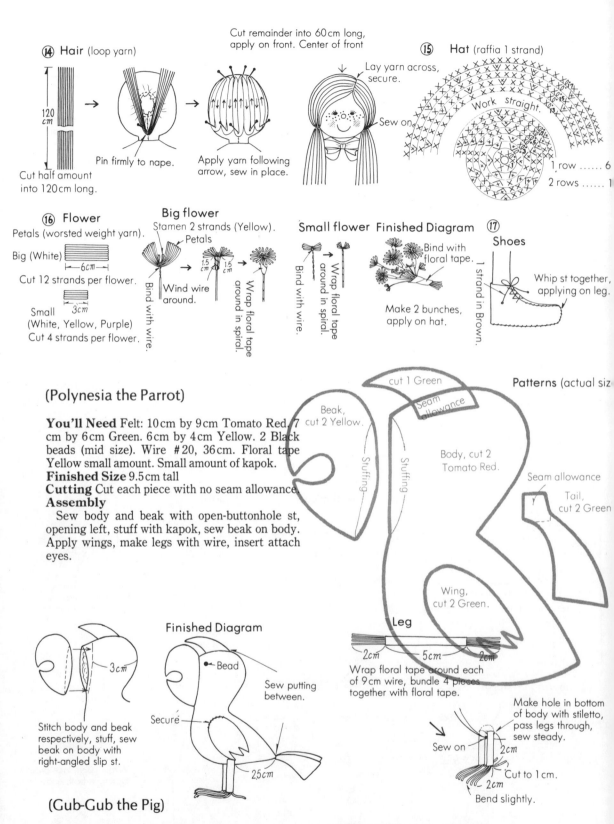

⑭ Hair (loop yarn)

120 cm

Cut half amount into 120cm long.

Pin firmly to nape.

Apply yarn following arrow, sew in place.

Cut remainder into 60cm long, apply on front. Center of front

Lay yarn across, secure.

Sew on

⑮ Hat (raffia 1 strand)

Work straight.

1 row 6
2 rows 1

⑯ Flower
Petals (worsted weight yarn).

Big (White)
├─6cm─┤

Cut 12 strands per flower.

Small
(White, Yellow, Purple)
Cut 4 strands per flower.
├─3cm─┤

Big flower
Stamen 2 strands (Yellow).
Petals

Bind with wire.

Wind wire around.

1.5 cm 1.5 cm

Wrap floral tape around in spiral.

Bind with wire.

Wrap floral tape around in spiral.

Small flower

Bind with wire.

Finished Diagram

Bind with floral tape.

Make 2 bunches, apply on hat.

⑰ Shoes

1 strand in Brown.

Whip st together, applying on leg.

(Polynesia the Parrot)

You'll Need Felt: 10cm by 9cm Tomato Red. 7 cm by 6cm Green. 6cm by 4cm Yellow. 2 Black beads (mid size). Wire #20, 36cm. Floral tape Yellow small amount. Small amount of kapok.
Finished Size 9.5cm tall
Cutting Cut each piece with no seam allowance.
Assembly
  Sew body and beak with open-buttonhole st, opening left, stuff with kapok, sew beak on body. Apply wings, make legs with wire, insert attach eyes.

Patterns (actual siz

cut 1 Green

Beak, cut 2 Yellow.

Seam allowance

Stuffing

Stuffing

Body, cut 2 Tomato Red.

Seam allowance
Tail, cut 2 Green

Wing, cut 2 Green.

Leg

2cm — 5cm — 2cm

Wrap floral tape around each of 9cm wire, bundle 4 pieces together with floral tape.

Make hole in bottom of body with stiletto, pass legs through, sew steady.

Sew on

2cm

Cut to 1cm.

2cm

Bend slightly.

Finished Diagram

3cm

Stitch body and beak respectively, stuff, sew beak on body with right-angled slip st.

Bead

Sew putting between.

Secure

2.5cm

(Gub-Gub the Pig)

You'll Need Felt 20cm square Pink, 6cm square LightPink. 6-strand embroidery floss Yellow, Dark Brown, sewing cotton Black small amount each. 10g. kapok. Glue.

Finished Size Refer to chart.
Cutting Cut each piece with no seam allowance.
Assembly
  Felt pieces are sewn with open-buttonhole stitch.

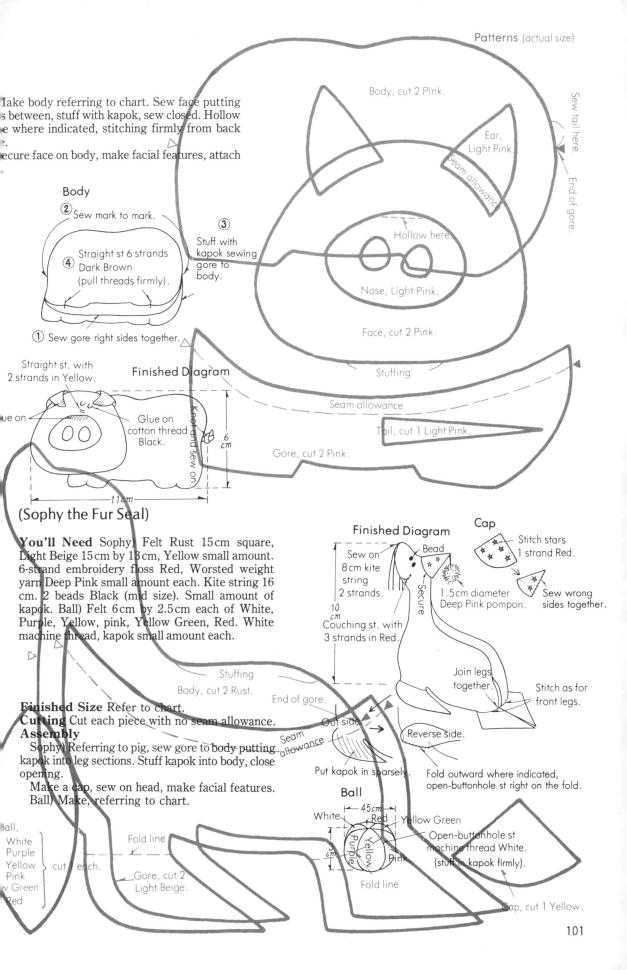

Patterns (actual size)

Body, cut 2 Pink.

Sew tail here.

End of gore.

Ear, Light Pink.

Seam allowance

Make body referring to chart. Sew face putting
between, stuff with kapok, sew closed. Hollow
where indicated, stitching firmly from back

ecure face on body, make facial features, attach

Hollow here.

Body

② Sew mark to mark.

③ Stuff with kapok sewing gore to body.

④ Straight st 6 strands Dark Brown (pull threads firmly).

① Sew gore right sides together.

Nose, Light Pink.

Face, cut 2 Pink.

Straight st. with 2 strands in Yellow.

Finished Diagram

ue on

Glue on cotton thread Black.

6 cm

Knot and sew on.

Stuffing

Seam allowance

Tail, cut 1 Light Pink.

Gore, cut 2 Pink.

11 cm

(Sophy the Fur Seal)

You'll Need Sophy) Felt Rust 15 cm square,
Light Beige 15 cm by 13 cm, Yellow small amount.
6-strand embroidery floss Red, Worsted weight
yarn Deep Pink small amount each. Kite string 16
cm. 2 beads Black (mid size). Small amount of
kapok. Ball) Felt 6 cm by 2.5 cm each of White,
Purple, Yellow, pink, Yellow Green, Red. White
machine thread, kapok small amount each.

Finished Diagram

Sew on 8 cm kite string 2 strands.

10 cm

Couching st. with 3 strands in Red.

Bead

Secure

Cap

Stitch stars 1 strand Red.

1.5 cm diameter Deep Pink pompon.

Sew wrong sides together.

Join legs together.

Stitch as for front legs.

Stuffing

Body, cut 2 Rust.

End of gore.

Cut side.

Seam allowance

Reverse side.

Finished Size Refer to chart.
Cutting Cut each piece with no seam allowance.
Assembly
 Sophy) Referring to pig, sew gore to body putting
kapok into leg sections. Stuff kapok into body, close
opening.
 Make a cap, sew on head, make facial features.
 Ball) Make, referring to chart.

Put kapok in sparsely.

Fold outward where indicated, open-buttonhole st right on the fold.

Ball

White
Red
Yellow Green
Purple
Yellow
Pink

4.5 cm

3 cm

Open-buttonhole st machine thread White. (stuff in kapok firmly).

Ball,
White
Purple
Yellow
Pink
w Green
Red

cut each.

Fold line

Gore, cut 2 Light Beige.

Fold line

Cap, cut 1 Yellow.

The Little Prince

(Little Prince)

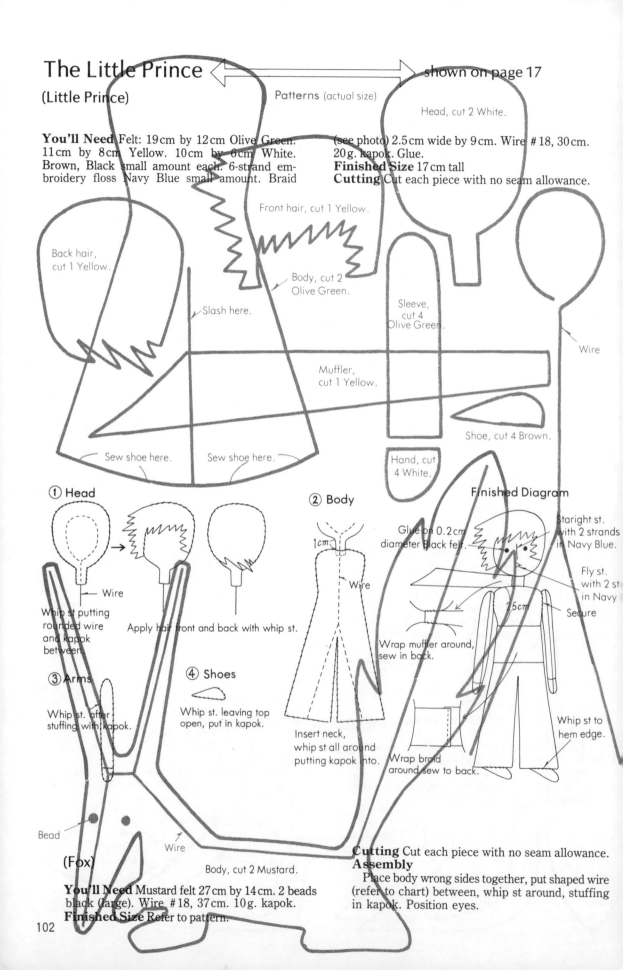

Patterns (actual size)

shown on page 17

Head, cut 2 White.

You'll Need Felt: 19 cm by 12 cm Olive Green. 11 cm by 8 cm Yellow. 10 cm by 6 cm White. Brown, Black small amount each. 6-strand embroidery floss Navy Blue small amount. Braid (see photo) 2.5 cm wide by 9 cm. Wire #18, 30 cm. 20 g. kapok. Glue.
Finished Size 17 cm tall
Cutting Cut each piece with no seam allowance.

Front hair, cut 1 Yellow.

Back hair, cut 1 Yellow.

Body, cut 2 Olive Green.

Slash here.

Sleeve, cut 4 Olive Green.

Wire

Muffler, cut 1 Yellow.

Shoe, cut 4 Brown.

Sew shoe here.   Sew shoe here.

Hand, cut 4 White.

① Head

Wire

Whip st putting rounded wire and kapok between.

Apply hair front and back with whip st.

③ Arms

Whip st. after stuffing with kapok.

② Body

1 cm

Wire

Insert neck, whip st all around putting kapok into.

④ Shoes

Whip st. leaving top open, put in kapok.

Finished Diagram

Glue on 0.2 cm diameter Black felt.

Staright st. with 2 strands in Navy Blue.

Fly st. with 2 st in Navy

2.5 cm

Secure

Wrap muffler around, sew in back.

Wrap braid around sew to back.

Whip st to hem edge.

Bead

Wire

(Fox)

Body, cut 2 Mustard.

You'll Need Mustard felt 27 cm by 14 cm. 2 beads black (large). Wire #18, 37 cm. 10 g. kapok.
Finished Size Refer to pattern.

Cutting Cut each piece with no seam allowance.
Assembly
   Place body wrong sides together, put shaped wire (refer to chart) between, whip st around, stuffing in kapok. Position eyes.

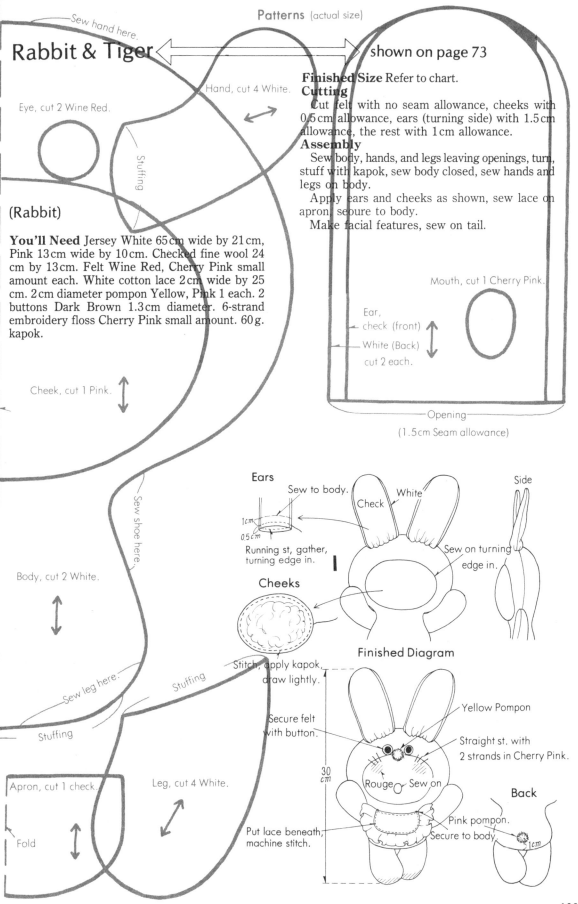

Patterns (actual size)

Rabbit & Tiger

shown on page 73

Sew hand here.

Eye, cut 2 Wine Red.

Hand, cut 4 White.

Stuffing

(Rabbit)

You'll Need Jersey White 65 cm wide by 21 cm, Pink 13 cm wide by 10 cm. Checked fine wool 24 cm by 13 cm. Felt Wine Red, Cherry Pink small amount each. White cotton lace 2 cm wide by 25 cm. 2 cm diameter pompon Yellow, Pink 1 each. 2 buttons Dark Brown 1.3 cm diameter. 6-strand embroidery floss Cherry Pink small amount. 60 g. kapok.

Finished Size Refer to chart.
Cutting
Cut felt with no seam allowance, cheeks with 0.5 cm allowance, ears (turning side) with 1.5 cm allowance, the rest with 1 cm allowance.
Assembly
Sew body, hands, and legs leaving openings, turn, stuff with kapok, sew body closed, sew hands and legs on body.
Apply ears and cheeks as shown, sew lace on apron, secure to body.
Make facial features, sew on tail.

Mouth, cut 1 Cherry Pink.

Ear,
check (front)
White (Back)
cut 2 each.

Opening
(1.5 cm Seam allowance)

Cheek, cut 1 Pink.

Sew shoe here.

Body, cut 2 White.

Ears

Sew to body.
Check   White

1cm
0.5cm

Running st, gather,
turning edge in.

Side

Sew on turning
edge in.

Cheeks

Sew leg here.

Stuffing

Stuffing

Stitch, apply kapok,
draw lightly.

Finished Diagram

Secure felt
with button.

Yellow Pompon

Straight st. with
2 strands in Cherry Pink.

30
cm

Rouge   Sew on

Back

Apron, cut 1 check.

Leg, cut 4 White.

Fold

Put lace beneath;
machine stitch.

Pink pompon.
Secure to body.

1cm

103

(Tiger)

You'll Need Jersey striped 72 cm wide by 21 cm, Cream 13 cm wide by 10 cm, Yellow 15 cm wide by 6 cm. White felt small amount. 2 cm diameter Green pompon. 2 buttons Black 1.3 cm diameter. 6-strand embroidery floss Red, Black small amount each. 60 g. kapok.
Finished Size Refer to chart.
Cutting
Cut felt with no seam allowance, cheeks with 0.5 cm allowance, the rest with 1 cm allowance.

Body & hands stripe
Cheeks Cream } Same Pattern as rabbit.
Eyes White

Patterns (actual size)

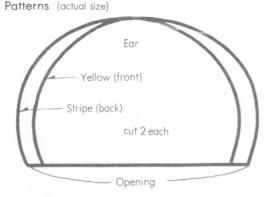

Ear

— Yellow (front)

— Stripe (back)

cut 2 each

— Opening

Assembly

Sew hands and legs on body as for rabbit. Sew tail leaving opening, turn, put kapok into top end only, sew on body. Sew ears, turn, gather as shown, secure in place. Attach cheeks as for rabbit.
Make facial features referring to chart.

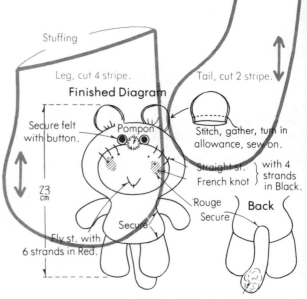

Stuffing

Stuffing

Leg, cut 4 stripe.

Tail, cut 2 stripe.

Finished Diagram

Secure felt with button.

Pompon

Stitch, gather, turn in allowance, sew on.

Straight st. French knot } with 4 strands in Black.

Rouge Secure

Back

Secure

23 cm

Fly st. with 6 strands in Red.

Put kapok lightly into top end.

Continued from page 59.

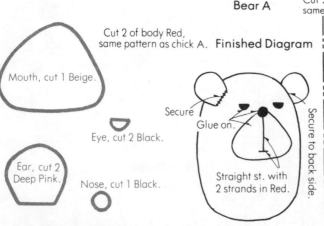

Bear A

Cut 2 of body Red, same pattern as chick A. **Finished Diagram**

Mouth, cut 1 Beige.

Eye, cut 2 Black.

Ear, cut 2 Deep Pink.

Nose, cut 1 Black.

Secure

Glue on.

Straight st. with 2 strands in Red.

Cut 2 of body Blue, same pattern as chick A.
1 of mouth Beige,
2 of ear Navy Blue,
1 of nose Black.

2 of eye Black, same pattern as nose of bear A.

Secure to back side.

Bear B
Finished Diagram
Patterns same as bear A.

Glue on.

Secu

Straight st. with 2 strands in Red.

Secure to back side.

Doll (pair) ⟵⟶ shown on page 25

You'll Need (for each) White rayon 60 cm by 30 cm. Cotton pile Light Beige 50 cm by 30 cm. Crepe de chine Navy Blue small amount. 6-strand embroidery floss Pink small amount. 60 g. packing. 35 g. tetoron batting. 20 g. cotton batting. Glue. Boy) Striped cotton 47 cm by 14 cm. Blue denim 45 cm by 16 cm. Sport weight yarn 20 g. Yellow Brown. White machine thread small amount. 2 buttons Blue 0.8 cm diameter. Girl) Orange cotton

47 cm by 14 cm. Floral print Orange 64 cm by 11 cm. Sport weight yarn 30 g. Yellow Brown. Ribbon Dusty Green 0.4 cm wide by 25 cm. Elastic 18 cm.
Finished Size 32 cm tall
Cutting
Cut rayon and cotton pile with allowance indicated, the rest with 1 cm allowance.

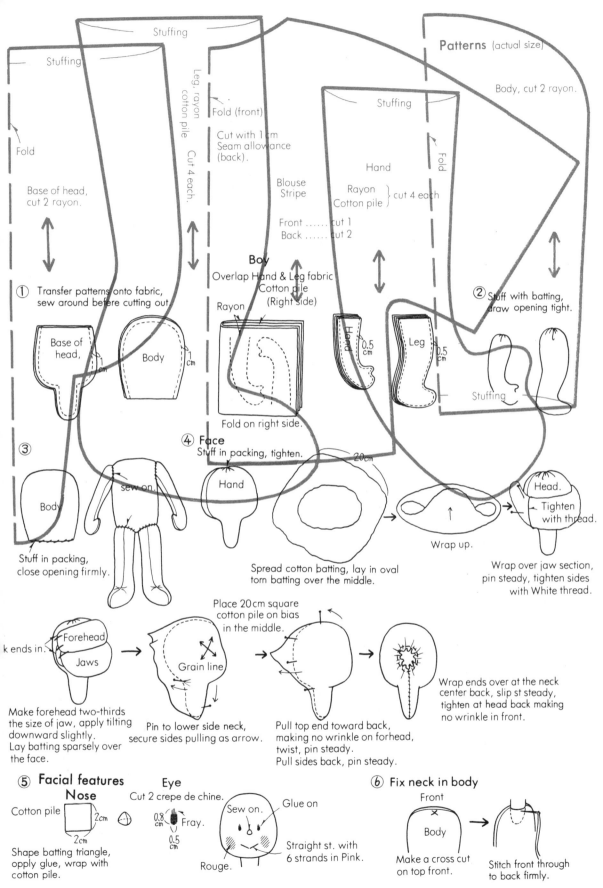

Stuffing

Stuffing

Fold

Base of head,
cut 2 rayon.

Leg, rayon
cotton pile

Cut 4 each.

Fold (front)

Cut with 1 cm
Seam allowance
(back).

Blouse
Stripe

Front ...... cut 1
Back ...... cut 2

Boy
Overlap Hand & Leg fabric
Cotton pile
(Right side)

Rayon

Stuffing

Hand

Rayon
Cotton pile } cut 4 each

Fold

Patterns (actual size)

Body, cut 2 rayon.

① Transfer patterns onto fabric,
sew around before cutting out.

② Stuff with batting,
draw opening tight.

Base of
head,
1 cm

Body
1 cm

Rayon

Hand
0.5 cm

Leg
0.5 cm

Stuffing

Fold on right side.

③

Body

Stuff in packing,
close opening firmly.

sew on.

④ **Face**
Stuff in packing, tighten.

Hand

20cm

Wrap up.

Spread cotton batting, lay in oval
torn batting over the middle.

Head.

Tighten
with thread.

Wrap over jaw section,
pin steady, tighten sides
with White thread.

k ends in.

Forehead

Jaws

Make forehead two-thirds
the size of jaw, apply tilting
downward slightly.
Lay batting sparsely over
the face.

Place 20cm square
cotton pile on bias
in the middle.

Grain line

Pin to lower side neck,
secure sides pulling as arrow.

Pull top end toward back,
making no wrinkle on forhead,
twist, pin steady.
Pull sides back, pin steady.

Wrap ends over at the neck
center back, slip st steady,
tighten at head back making
no wrinkle in front.

⑤ **Facial features**
Nose

Cotton pile

2cm
2cm

Shape batting triangle,
opply glue, wrap with
cotton pile.

Eye
Cut 2 crepe de chine.

0.8 cm
Fray.
0.5 cm

Sew on.
Glue on

Straight st. with
6 strands in Pink.

Rouge.

⑥ **Fix neck in body**

Front

Body

Make a cross cut
on top front.

Stitch front through
to back firmly.

105

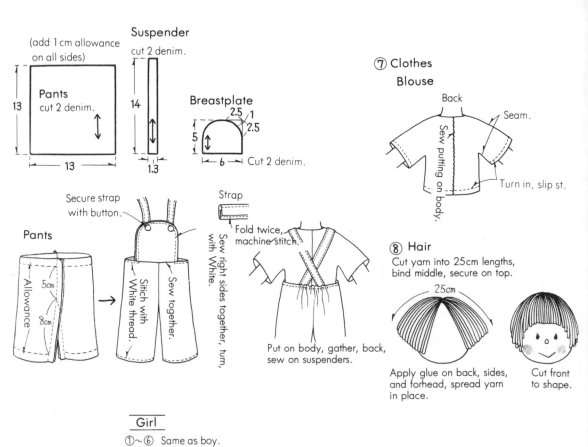

(add 1 cm allowance on all sides)

Suspender
cut 2 denim.

Pants
cut 2 denim.

13

14

13

1.3

Breastplate
2.5 — 1
2.5
5
— 6 — Cut 2 denim.

⑦ Clothes
Blouse
Back
Seam.
Sew putting on body.
Turn in, slip st.

Pants

Secure strap with button.

Allowance
5cm
8cm
Stitch with White thread.
Sew together.

Strap
Fold twice, machine stitch.
Sew right sides together, turn, with White.
Put on body, gather, back, sew on suspenders.

⑧ Hair
Cut yarn into 25cm lengths, bind middle, secure on top.
25cm
Apply glue on back, sides, and forhead, spread yarn in place.
Cut front to shape.

Girl

①~⑥ Same as boy.
(Make facial features referring to photo.)

⑦ Clothes
(Add 1.5cm allowance on top side of skirt, 1 cm allowance on remaining sides.)

8
Skirt cut 1 floral print.
34

9
Pants cut 2 floral print.
12

Pants
4cm
5cm
* Make blouse with Orange as for boy.

Tuck and secure to body.
Running st, gather to leg.

Skirt
Fold back allowance, stitch casing pass elastic through.
8 cm
Turn twice, slip st.
1cm
Sew end together

⑧ Hair
Cut yarn into 36cm lengths, bind and apply.
36cm
Apply glue on back, sides, and forhead, position yarn.
Trim front.

Attach ribbon.

Finished Diagram

Doll (pair in glasses)

← shown on page 45

Patterns (actual size)

(Boy)

You'll Need Cotton jersey Brown 47cm wide by 25cm. Ribbed cotton Reddish Purple 32cm wide by 25cm. Cotton print Yellow 18cm by 13cm. Felt Blue 8cm by 7cm, Brown 6cm by 5cm, Green small amount. Brown leather 19cm by 3cm. 6-strand embroidery floss Black, Red small amount each. Lightweight yarn Black small amount.

Yellow wire #20, 22cm. 5 of splittable chopstick. Packing, kapok small amount each. Glue.
Finished Size 47cm tall
Cutting
Cut head, nose, bodice, and pants with 1cm seam allowance, the rest with no allowance.

Buckle cut 1 leather.

Bodice cut 2 print.

Pants, cut 2 Red Purple.

Shoe, cut 4 Blue.

4 of head jersey,
1 of nose jersey,
4 of palm felt Brown.
} Patterns Same as boy on page 46.

Glasses same as for girl.

①.② Same as boy on page 46.

③ Hair (lightweight yarn)

Wind 70 times around middle 3 fingers. Make 3 portions.

Back

Apply glue on head, spread into 3 rows, steady in shape.

④ Bodice

Insert neck here.

2cm

1.5 cm

Hand Make as for boy on page 47

Sew right sides together, inserting hands, turn.

Leg

3cm Jersey

25 cm Stick

21cm

1cm

6cm

1.5cm

Sew steady.

0.5 cm

2cm

Stitch.

Sew to bodice.

Glue 2 pieces together.

Stuff kapok lightly, insert neck and legs.

⑤ Pants

Clip

Sew right sides together, turn.

Turn hem up, glue steady.

Belt, cut 1 leather

2

16

Collar, cut 1 Green

1.5

5

Finished Diagram

Bullion st. with 3 strands in Black.

Apply as for girl.

Draw with Red pencil.

Make as for boy on page 47.

Glue steady.

Straight st with 3 strands in Red.

Glue steady.

Make as for boy on page 47.

107

(Girl)

You'll Need Cotton jersey Off-White 47 cm wide by 18 cm. Gingham checked with Red and White 34 cm by 17 cm. Felt: 7 cm by 4 cm Deep Pink. 6 cm by 5 cm each of Light Pink, Green. Red small amount. 6-strand embroidery floss Red, Black small amount each. Sport weight yarn Dark Brown small amount. Red ribbon 0.4 cm wide by 30 cm. Yellow wire #20, 22 cm. 5 of splittable chopstick. Packing, kapok small amount each. Glue.

Finished Size 42 cm tall

Cutting

Cut head, nose, and dress with 1 cm seam allowance, the rest with no allowance.

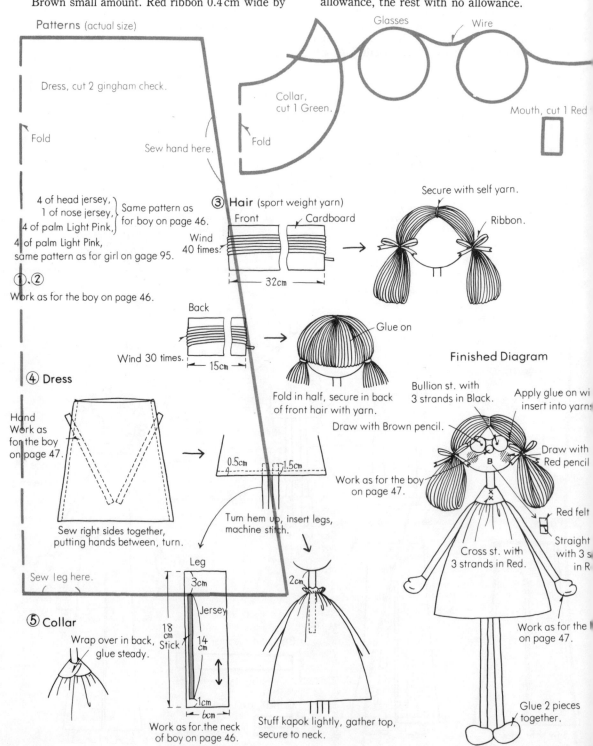

Patterns (actual size)

Glasses   Wire

Dress, cut 2 gingham check.

Collar, cut 1 Green.

Mouth, cut 1 Red

Fold

Fold

Sew hand here.

③ Hair (sport weight yarn)

4 of head jersey,
1 of nose jersey,
4 of palm Light Pink,
4 of palm Light Pink,
same pattern as for girl on gage 95.

Same pattern as for boy on page 46.

Front   Cardboard

Wind 40 times.

— 32cm —

Secure with self yarn.

Ribbon.

①.②

Work as for the boy on page 46.

Back

Wind 30 times.   — 15cm —

Glue on

Finished Diagram

④ Dress

Hand Work as for the boy on page 47.

Fold in half, secure in back of front hair with yarn.

Bullion st. with 3 strands in Black.

Apply glue on wi insert into yarns

Draw with Brown pencil.

Draw with Red pencil

0.5cm   1.5cm

Work as for the boy on page 47.

Red felt

Sew right sides together, putting hands between, turn.

Turn hem up, insert legs, machine stitch.

Cross st. with 3 strands in Red.

Straight with 3 s in R

Sew leg here.

Leg

2cm

Sew leg here.

3cm

Jersey

Work as for the on page 47.

⑤ Collar

Wrap over in back, glue steady.

18 cm   Stick   14 cm

1cm
— 6cm —

Work as for the neck of boy on page 46.

Stuff kapok lightly, gather top, secure to neck.

Glue 2 pieces together.

Some Hints for Stuffed Toys

Materials

Try to find materials of your own in your daily life. All those old clothes in your wardrobe, ribbon tape or vinyl string used for packages, left-over pieces of yarn or fabric, etc., can all be used to create delightful toys.

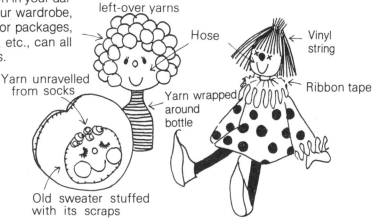

Pompons of left-over yarns

Hose

Vinyl string

Yarn unravelled from socks

Ribbon tape

Yarn wrapped around bottle

Old sweater stuffed with its scraps

Cutting

Transfer pattern on tracing paper, cut out the traced pattern. Place the pattern on fabric, with its arrow mark parallel to the grain of fabric, trace outline using tailor's chalk.

Cut fabric along the inside of chalk line. Be careful not to cut the pieces for left and right in the same direction.

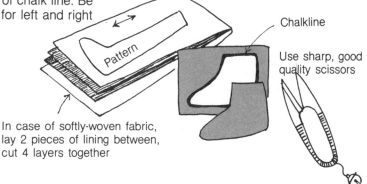

Pattern

Chalkline

Use sharp, good quality scissors

In case of softly-woven fabric, lay 2 pieces of lining between, cut 4 layers together

Sewing

With seam allowance...Machine stitch wrong sides together. In the case of hand sewing, work fine back stitches using heavier weight of sewing cotton.

Without seam allowance (felt for instance)...Putting pieces right sides out, work around in open-buttonhole stitch or whip stitch, using machine thread or 6-strand embroidery floss in matching color.

Open-buttonhole stitch

Whip stitch

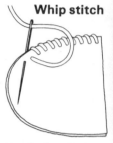

Right-angled slip stitch

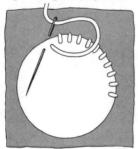

Securing fabric piece with open-buttonhole stitch

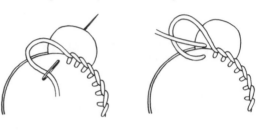

Turning inside (right side) out

Trim allowance to 0.5cm-0.8cm, clip at intervals, turn the piece to right side.

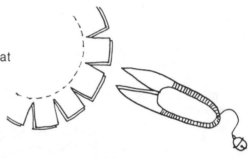

Stuffing Materials

Kapok..The most suitable material for these stuffed crafts, both for the comfortable way it feels and the natural way it springs back into shape. Stuff it in firmly from the beginning, or the work will get thinner in use.

Tetoron batting...Springy, washable, and not stiff like cotton batting, it is a very convenient stuffing, and one of the most popular ones.

Packing...A kind of wooden chip, it might be called "wood wool." It is convenient to use for sections like the head and body, where a solid finish is required.

Stuffing Methods

Do not stuff any piece of material rounded by hand. Fray material softly and build up an area little by little. If a narrower section is to be stuffed, use a screwdriver, chopstick, or some similar kind of stick. As for the neck, stuff plenty of padding into it tightly, or insert a piece of thick wire or stick in the middle, so that the head above becomes stable.

Having finished stuffing the work, tap the whole work with your palm to make the padding inside smooth. Finish the work by ironing with a damp pressing cloth.

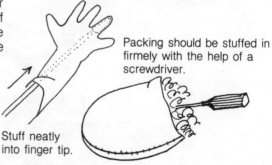

Packing should be stuffed in firmly with the help of a screwdriver.

Stuff neatly into finger tip.

Setting Hands and Legs in Position

Secure with fine stitches scooping the sections inward.

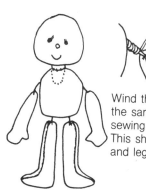

Wind thread around the same way as sewing on buttons. This shanklets hands and legs move freely.

Stitches Used in the Work

Outline stitch

out
1
3 out
2 in

Chain stitch

Cross stitch

Straight stitch

1 out 3 out
2 4

Double cross stitch

Fly stitch

1 out
2 in
3 out
4 in

French knot stitch

2 in
1 out
2 in
1 out
1 out 2 in

side view   top view

Bullion stitch

3 out
out
2 in
4 in

Bullion knot stitch

Couching stitch

9 7 5 3 out out
8 6 4 2 1

Satin stitch

1 3 out
out 2 in

111